There is no truth greater than ourselves.

Electric Loser Land

♋

How to read The American Homeless Companion

If you are reading this sentence you are not a normal person, so *The American Homeless Companion* is not a normal book.

This is an account of what could have been my terrifying decent into the life-ending predicament of homelessness. When I began this book, I thought that was the only story there was about homelessness. Two years into this work it became clear that I had been utterly wrong. That almost everyone looking at homelessness, including the homeless, were fundamentally clueless about the actual state of homelessness in America, the reason for homelessness, and how homelessness is a long-sought prize for civilization. A gift we overlook, and resist being educated about in ways that aren't prejudicial.

By year three I was fluent in the organization and politics within the ranks of the homeless. Real forces that are awakened by a closer bond to the Earth and a separation from the concepts of time and calendaring became evident. An arsenal of forces and stations of mind, as simple as magic and regularly harnessed by homeless people, began to work for me too, now a completely committed veteran of homeless society. My homeless brothers and sisters, all family, didn't share common terms to describe the changes they felt as homelessness sunk in. Didn't share common labels for events like: When stuff simply appears when you need it. Allowing the body to work separately from the mind. The reversal of self-actualization absent of time and material wealth.

I went to naming these events. Dense Now, Natural

Providership, The Crossroads of Commitment, and I renamed, or more properly defined, often excused and marginalizing terms like homelessness, housing, satisfaction, and people.

What appeared before me was no longer a state of homelessness, by any measure. Even not having a home. What I'd become was a citizen occupying an added rung to the economic ladder. A yet to be legitimized layer of citizens leading relatively healthy and happy lives right below our current economic layer made up of those living in what's defined as poverty. I was part of the big example that the society I lived in was a successful, healthy, prosperous, and liberating project. It took a long time to build along an ugly road, but it's built and it works. We have built and perfected things to the point that we have extra people who society doesn't need to do anything but eat, love, be safe, and acquire their own destinies. We should consider this milestone triumphant. Did primitive man and its cultural founders aim for a future where their tribe is forever shackled in labor, constantly worried about food and supplies, and held-up by a criminal pay-for-shelter industrial complex? Where disease, famine, poor drinking water and child mortality stifle our ability to grow our ranks and prosper?

No way.

No matter how many lashes cut through the backs of workers in order to transport granite from the quarries to the temple's construction site, eons of bad bosses and slave labor conditions didn't obstruct the original utopia vision of society in its completeness. A vision that was top down. Always with a destination in mind that tells us it's okay to stop working so hard. We've got it folks, it's done. Just look around. Nothing else to do, really. The gamification of things already thought up and working. Labor rolls there only to prevent homelessness, when it comes right down to the real boogie man that keeps people in jobs they have no interest in, working.

We're there now. Homelessness is the proof, not the problem. How wonderful it is too know our society is mature enough for those born with no nagging ambition only love have an economic layer that validates them doing nothing. Nothing, instead of monkeying up someone others dream or place business because they are told they have to work there, or a boss it forced to hire them. A legitimate place on the economic ladder you can go to if you disagree with the CEO so badly that you resign. You probably wouldn't have spoken up to the CEO had you been worried about becoming homeless. Take off. Do nothing. Come back when you want to.

This is the promise, the unopened gift of what should not be called homelessness.

I tried Baseline on for size, my homeless friends loved it. They could now consider themselves Baseliners, living completely free and satisfied lives just beneath institutionalized poverty. Baseline, and Status, all the upward rungs on the economic ladder, rich or poor, anything above poverty enters Status. Makes it easy. Strips away any pre-judgements that limit our thinking and criminalize a growing population in our society.

There is no homeless problem. There are no homeless people. Only an made up enemy of industrialization, as defined by *The American Homeless Companion.*

The way out is in front of us right now. The key is our inability to accept of loss. We must mature as people to a point where we can accept loss. Accept loss forever. *The American Homeless Companion* will show you why this matters, and why it's been invisible to us up to now.

It will also ask this of you: Become homeless. Take this book along with the clothes on your back and walk out the door with what ever's in your purse or pocket. That's it.

As you enter Baseline, you will look back at Status

society and see the equivalent of a strict boarding school for children who still maintain the school's archaic code of conduct, its rules of order, and its punishments for wrong doing. The children smile but something is missing. Everything they do is inconclusive. Absent of loss and needed closure. Everything falling short of finality, be it a big issue or a minor one. What haunts this misery is the children do not realize that the adult school masters have left the building. Are gone. Long gone. These children – you, with your job - accept their condition because they have never been shown anything else. It is not their fault. They are being good. Doing what they were taught was right. They resist change, but they are just children, or soon to be former children.

When I entered Baseline and looked back at Status, I fell upon the infinity of three words. I didn't feel like thinking about anything more. I was homeless. Accept loss forever.

"Accept loss forever" is entry number 19 on a list of 30 recommendations which author Jack Kerouac titled *Belief & Technique for Modern Prose*. It was published in 1958.

Compared to the other 29 drifting and poetic recommendations on Kerouac's list, such as number 12: "In tranced fixation dreaming upon object before you." Or number 24: "No fear or shame in the dignity of yr experience, language & knowledge." Number 19 is odd in its finality. It's in the perfect format of a Jeopardy answer:

"What is accept loss forever? Solutions for Mankind for a thousand, Alex..."

So, if number 19 is a Jeopardy answer, what was the question?

The American Homeless Companion believes that Jack Kerouac answered an all-important question for mankind with the line "accept loss forever" before he understood what the question was. Kerouac naturally stumbled on an attractive poetic answer to something that had to be important, but then left it there. His actions did not display an understanding of the enormity of the poetic question that his script begged, nor its urgency. And he didn't afford himself enough time to figure it out. The author of On the Road didn't believe anyone cared, so he died at 47.

In May 2014 I celebrated my 50th birthday with friends, neighbors and acquaintances, each of whom called some part of San Francisco's immense and sprawling Golden Gate Park their home.

From this family of so-called homeless people I'd witnessed the unbearable truth that we have shaped ourselves into a society that by absolutely no fault of our own is a society that cannot accept loss. We are a frightfully successful society that mistakenly remains unable to let anything go. We'd be dust already without this irrefutable reflex. The advantages of no ending, the permanence of no conclusiveness, the safety of no loss, are all just as real as their associated horrors.

I thought if Kerouac's #19 is a Jeopardy answer, maybe this is the clue:

"It's the idea we all should embrace in order to enjoy what we have, not build what we don't. Thirty seconds. Good luck."

♋

The American Homeless Companion

The American Homeless Companion, Second printing

51 Sixth Street
San Francisco, California 94103
ISBN-13: 978-1497312319

"Homeless" poem by Kelly Grabianowsk

For Harriet Kilgore

♋

The Ten Recommends
of Homelessness

Always wait
Always be polite
Always be truthful
Always radiate the wise
Always avoid childishness
Always watch the weather
Always have something else to do
Always be yourself, not the people you need
Always confront prejudice with truth's sympathy
Never just take

♋

In January 2014, after surviving an apocalyptic divorce in New York and barely making it back to my beloved home city of San Francisco, I was given less than one hour to surrender my key and get the fuck out of a house on Potrero Hill which I'd dreamed would be home for the rest of my life, even though I wasn't supposed to be there.

So as I dreamed it was just a matter of time. Seven months of on-time rent paying and roustabouts with three roommates to break the only house rule: Don't even get close to having everyone kicked out by the landlord.

Don't make a fuss. Don't ask the landlord to fix anything. Never open the door unless they're calling from outside on their cell phone. Don't be late on rent. And remember: You don't live here. If the landlord sees you and asks, you're our friend who has his own place in the Sunset. Got it?

This was the Devil's bargain I jumped on, which kept our rent at a surreal $350 a month each. An unspeakable number for San Francisco, a city being drowned by its third and most powerful wave of hi-tech gentrification.

Realistically affordable housing like ours was traded in secret in San Francisco. Anyone posting a Craig's List ad that advertised room for rent, Potrero Hill, 4-bedroom house, pets, smoking okay, walk to Castro, Mission, $350/mo, no deposit) would get their inbox clogged for months with "Still available?" subject lines. Any applicant would tell us anything we wanted to hear to get the key.

If say, we lost a roomie and we remaining three conspired to keep the true monthly rent a secret in order to charge an incoming roommate market rate for the open room, say $1,200 per month, all we'd be asking for was a deep-pocketed applicant who would demand to be on the lease for that money. Dust off the lease and suddenly everyone pays $1,200 a month.

"Never call the landlord! We don't exist."

I repaired a doorknob that fell to the hallway floor when a vacuum ran past it. An eighty-nine cent hex key from a hardware store on Castro Street was all it took.

"By the way, how long has that doorknob in the hallway been falling off?"

"I don't know. Probably since I moved in," the primary lease holder said. His name was Steve. I cared about him, because I'd known him for 23 years – the same length of time that Steve had lived at the Potrero Hill house.

This means that Steve's landlord, our landlord, hadn't been called to repair or replace anything since the Clinton era - An economic expansion fueled by Silicon Valley technology companies whose well-paid employees set off a bidding war for San Francisco real estate already in a choke hold of limited acreage and supply.

Tragically, there had not been a comfortable time for rent-controlled tenants in San Francisco to call their landlord to fix something since *Smells Like Teen Spirit* debuted on MTV.

The elegance of our unrestored Potrero Hill Victorian, the magnificence of our location, our panoramic views, and the money we saved on rent so we could enjoy the cost of San Francisco was worth putting up with a house where nothing worked except the electrical outlets. If you reached for an on/off switch or a button designed into the 70-year old woodwork it did nothing. We carried flashlights through the long, pitch black hallways. We walked around in blankets to stay warm.

We supported the unacceptable by putting up with it. We endured squatter-level amenities that would appear irrational if you examined our resumes.

But behavior in that house was terrifyingly rational. Rational because the beliefs, fears, and preferences that the threat of homelessness enforced among us were consistent in all other parts of our lives. Nobel Prize winning economist Daniel Kahneman has written that "A rational person can believe in ghosts so long as all her other beliefs are consistent with the existence of ghosts."

The ghost on Potrero Hill was an unseen landlord who bathed in blood and perched outside with a shredded lease in its claws, itching to raise the rent by $3,000 if he recognized your phone number in his "missed calls" folder.

This ghost haunted our jobs, goals, love lives and self-esteem. It wasn't rent. It was a heartbeat. A pump to all points supporting life. Without a place to live, everything withers and dies.

"Hi, guy," the landlord said to me.

I was handing out Halloween candy. Our front door was open. I was playing *The Monster Mash* real loud on repeat, making up bad jokes for spooky kids through the spittle of my cheap plastic vampire teeth.

"Everything okay in there?" the landlord asked me. He unlocked Sarah and Jim's apartment door and grabbed a yellow Craftsman toolbox set at the bottom of the staircase, which explained all the stake hammering upstairs. I sensed myself growing dead pale when I smiled through the fangs and nodded yes, "everything's okay."

"Happy Halloween, Jack Kerouac!" The Google Lawyer hollered at me gleefully as she crossed the street towards us with her 5-year old daughter who was Cinderella for the night.

I hung out with The Google Lawyer's unemployed husband during the day while she hustled to The Quad and back in her MINI Cooper. She was loaded with nice stories about me and gave me a great big hug.

"Best new neighbor ever!" she said all Halloween-loudly.

I sunk my vampire teeth into her neck.

January arrived.

"What are you talking about I have to leave now? You can't just throw me out of here. Who called the landlord?"

"The landlord called the girls. So they're both freaking out. They won't stand behind you. They're threatening to call the police if you make a stink about it."

The thought crossed my mind, but I didn't want to become the next San Francisco protester to ignore an eviction and dig in hard and well-defended under liberal San Francisco housing protections. These protesters become live-in pains in your ass for months, if not years. They get off scot-free, but leave behind zero friends.

That's right, you can just stop paying rent in San Francisco, and unlike a city such as Dallas or Miami where you'll be beaten to death for not paying rent, while the police cooperate in your beating, you can simply tell the San Francisco roommates who trusted you to fuck off, and expect no further checks from you. There is nothing they can do but go to court and huff and puff. Label their food and hide their beer.

Two Bay Area friends share similar horror stories of enduring the constant presence of a person who transforms into a total deadbeat stranger. Who cannot be locked out, kicked out, or verbally abused or it's a felony. Your felony.

"You're gonna make me homeless, you know that?"

"You just got paid. Get a hotel room. Call your sisters. Call your other friend."

I felt nothing. Thanks Steve.

My denial mechanism was shot, my credit rating was in negative numbers, my parents were dead, I was officially old, my resources were limited and my remaining friends were all protectively shacked up with wives who'd long ago stopped allowing an influence like mine to rub off on their alpha bread winners.

I felt nothing. Erased.

No person, no landmark, no moment comes to mind when I recall my walk from Potrero Hill into homelessness. A nondescript stroll into Golden Gate Park, into wilderness, without a picnic basket, family member or loved one. Carrying too much stuff to be leaving behind breadcrumbs.

♋

Definitions

People - Former children all equal in their determination to be truthful and compassionate to others, only wanting love, praise, freedom, piece of mind in their decisions and actions, and a culture that offers only good choices for those decisions and actions, not bad choices. <This definition of people applies in all references to the word no matter what station the person occupies. (i.e., there are no "bad" people, only bad choices from flawed systems).>

Satisfaction - The kinetic sensation of vanquished unhappiness. An in-cognizant, uneducated state of happiness. The apex of human sensation awareness at the desired state of absolute conclusion. Near total absence of desire, and its state upon which at total absence all desired past methods to achieve the state lose their desirability.

Baseline - Def. 1: The invalidated "basement" economic level below the lowest recognized level of Status <See definitions: Status.> on the socioeconomic scale. Absolute zero of Status.

Def. 2: The location or community where the occupants of Baseline live and the location of the only working social safety net.

Def. 3: A trend-neutral sense of well-being absent any obligation or dictate of Status. A state of personal autonomy from surrounding industrial systems and regulations. The calibration point for Satisfaction. <Formerly known as "homeless.">

Homeless - Def. 1: Nomads.

Def. 2: A divisive label designed to marginalize and dismiss discussion about American citizens who do not live in typical dwellings usable and transferable to another person. A buzz-word popularized by media and applied in prejudice to paint these Americans as unorganized hobos with no loyalty or integrity.

Def. 3: A global socioeconomic class of geographically dispersed communities composed of American citizens living healthy and productive lives below the lowest recognized economic Status.

Status – Def. 1: People living in industrial housing or paying rent for any form of dwelling or shelter. Collectively: Non-Baseliners.

Def.2: The physical location of all members of society not at Baseline.

Def. 3: An artificial measure of personal wealth, and state of constant alertness and attention to the protection and maintenance of ownership and possession. An assumed point along a measure of material wealth which affords access to all locations and material things at all points below it, but is denied free access to all locations and material things exclusive to Status levels above it.

Property - Anything that does not regenerate itself (i.e., a human is not property, nor Earth, nor a pear.) < The term "private property" is void on its assumption parts of Earth can be owned and that commerce cannot exist unless it is.>

Imagined Property - Outwardly extended social space that practitioners of possession and enforcement imagine exists beyond a valid property line at a distance in ratio with a person's material wealth. Area outside a person's control which is imagined to be.

< A home owner can get police to move a person from a public sidewalk.

A building owner can get people, cars, vendors, and signs moved from an entire area they do not own. A rich guy can call police 3000 miles away and say "I'm driving through the park with my daughter's fiancee this weekend and I don't want to see any homeless people." >

Dwelling - Any place a person dwells.

Shelter - Def. 1: An object of any size or shape that bears no expense or tax which all people have the inherent right to create at any time they choose. An object that people have privileges to utilize first, before all other animals or things. The location of Def. 1. Equally free from expense or tax or third party claim of ownership. < Definition implies shelter is not created on a dwelling already occupied by a shelter. >

Def. 2: Any natural or man-made structure created to be in the way of (a) what is carried by, and within the wind, (b) precipitation at any temperature, (c) light. < Shelter is not to be confused with any form of prevention device or mechanism to restrict free movement (i.e., a floor is not shelter, a door is not shelter. A window is shelter.) See Definitions: Fencing. Shelter is not a preventative until it is compounded into a state of insulation. >

Industrial Housing - Any shelter or dwelling created for the purpose of productization and resale, and held by third party claim of ownership for the purposes of financial income or like gain from its occupants. Any house, apartment, condominium, building, etc., created using industry and duplicated using similar materials. Industrial shelter created with integrated, flooring, fencing and insulation. Exclusionary property and imagined property designated to preserve moments in time and limit the introduction of change elements.

Fencing - Anything used to prohibit the free movement of moving things.

Dense Now - A person's observation at absolute present. A state of intensely heightened natural perception unobscured by interference from past or future thought. The experience of object permanence, where nothing new is interpreted beyond the singular event. Perception of one's environment after time and clocks are removed as measure and regulators of experience. How memories are recorded in Dense Now. < Think: The only state in which nothing new is going on.>

Natural Providership - The industry of Mother Nature as observed from a state of zero distraction. The surplus of natural cause and effect only available at and within Baseline. Earth's omnipresent force of becoming. A natural materialization mechanism metering the truth-adjusted frequency of opportunity measured from Dense Now. The provider of human necessity at Baseline.

The Crossroads of Commitment - The adjustment velocity required to depart conditions from any level of Status. A moment which arrives during a person's early acclimation from Status to Baseline defined by their realization that total commitment to Baseline society has becomes absolute. An event that relinquishes all efforts to depart Baseline at, or representing, any Status level other than that of Baseliner. The point of no return from the personal application of Baseline economics, not to the exclusion of other economic and personal theory that can be adjoined.

Industry - Def. 1: A perpetual motion formula meriting mankind divine Status for defying a physically impossible state. The non-organic manufacture, exchange and repetition engine delegated to take responsibility for non-stop refreshing of everything we do, wear, and use in some orderly manner we believe will be the most satisfying. A procedure with no end, no completion, no justification to stop as each exchange is an improvement on the last. A free and flexible bedazzlement shielded from blame by its inductive properties, thus prone to abuse by the control and trickery aspects of human belief systems. A man-made formula that operates on duplication of man-made goods designed for mass production of a single idea.

Def. 2: Mass production by machine which lowers product and design costs for purposes of greater accessibility. <Note: Industry excludes all things organic. Industry cannot increase or decrease organically. Industry is only an idea, not a thing. Just as knitting is a thing, not something you wear. You can wear a knit sweater but you do not say you are wearing knitting. Likewise you don't use industry, you use an industrial strength hammer. Industry can be neither bad, nor good.>

♋

Everything I Own
January 16, 2014

One pair of black Rockport laced shoes.
One biker-grade leather jacket.
One pair of black jeans.
One black T-shirt with an R. Crumb rendering of Jack Kerouac.
One gray wool sweater.
One black wool sweater.
Two pairs of underwear.
Two pairs of socks.
A backpack.
A Big River Outdoors sleeping bag.
A wooden cane.
An HP laptop, charger and mouse.
Three pairs of prescription glasses.
A small knife (really a nail file).
A pot pipe.
A cell phone (no smart anything).
A disk with a licensed copy of Windows Office software.
My New York drivers' license.
My expired passport.
A green Cross ballpoint pen that was my good luck charm as a cub reporter for Infoworld magazine.
A ballpoint pen with an embedded sound recorder storing the sound of my daughter saying her first word: "Da-da."
A small book my late Mother gave me titled *For My Son.*
And two PC drives I'd soon mail to a girlfriend in

Texas who told me they smelled like urine.

In addition, a friend of mine in New York protected an acoustic guitar my daughter put stickers all over for me, and a Bulova watch passed down to me from my Great Grandfather.

That's it. No bank account. No stuffed mattress, no nothing else to draw on, sell or liquidate.

Beneath my surrender bubbled a growing liberation from my destitution that dared me to lose what little left I had. Dump it all. That'll show 'em. After all I didn't care anymore. I *wanted* to be thrown out now. Fuck 'em. Embrace it.

I wasn't that overweight welfare case who, ignoring eviction, has to be carted out of his living room and into the street by four men shouldering the recliner he refuses to get out of. I refused to plead for shelter any further than I'd taken it with Steve, that asshole. I wasn't going to be standing outside the Potrero Hill door the next morning like a lost puppy. I would raise my middle finger to homelessness. Prove that it couldn't hurt or change me.

After three years of being beaten like a rat in a waste basket by Family Court I was so jaded and relinquished to failure that I really didn't give a shit about much anymore, least of all belongings and a place to put them. When you lose the things and people who've been load-bearing components to almost every aspect of your life, including your sanity, it's easy to let everything else go, just for the hell of it. It's fighting back by hurting yourself beyond everyone else's expectations. Those close to you see ruin and madness. It's possible for you not to care.

I a sick way, I was inspired by the darkest financial hours of my life. Yes, sick. Not purely romantic, this idea about shaking off the American Dream, being a free American in liberal San Francisco where the Hippies made their peace, love and whatever stand. Peace freak with a mean streak, even if the word Hippie had become code for bum.

Something had to keep me above the level I'd been thrown down to. My chin had to stay up. I walked into the Haight Street coffee shop Stanza, composed like housed San Franciscan carrying a backpack. My clothes were still spotless. Hair normal hipster bedhead. I sat at the counter, ordered a French press as it started to drizzle. I was indoors, staring out the window thinking I was special to be sitting there dry as homeless people walked by holding cheap plastic ponchos over their heads and gear, or totally soaked and unconcerned with it. I hadn't met a single one of them yet, but they were all much easier to spot than they'd been only a few hours ago. Before my self-image was called into check. How long could I keep buying coffee to sit in here every day on the $80 I had in my wallet? Or anywhere. How long could I afford shelter? There is no outside seating on upper Haight Street. No benches, and a flimsy unconstitutional law discourages sitting or laying down on the street. I had no camping gear. I was hungry now. No food for two days and the queezy stress of being kicked out.

From Stanza's storefront I spotted a discarded plastic bag beneath a parking meter. Sticking out was an opened container of Quaker Oatmeal, and what looked like an empty Snapple bottle. Leaving my backpack I slithered out the door and swept up the bag trying not to be noticed. Back inside I walked directly to the restroom where I was buzzed in. The oatmeal was a quarter full and dry. Hoping to find a hot water spigot on the sink it hit me I should have just asked for a cup of hot water up front. I was a freaking customer, after all.

I did, and the coffee jockey obliged, unmoved.

Keeping my prep work below the counter I poured the steaming water into the cardboard tube of oatmeal, which began dripping on my pants leg. Slow, fat scalding drops of oatmeal flavored H2O. I gave the water only seconds to absorb before turning around in my seat, gulping down the chewy under-cooked oatmeal, water dripping from both sides of my mouth I was swallowing so fast. It tasted excellent. I opened my eyes and saw a girl sitting down at the table nearest the counter. She watched me choke down the oatmeal as she lowered her purse to the floor an her butt to her seat. She was not impressed.

I turned back towards my empty coffee cup. I was still hungry, but the lump of under-cooked oats helped soothe the pang in my stomach. I'd done it. Eaten something thrown away by someone I didn't know. What did it matter? Only looks, and the details about me only I know. But eating garbage without a door key redefined everything about me, and everything I was coming in contact with. But it shouldn't have been that way. Nothing had happened, really. Five hours ago I was jacking off in bed listening to Tom Waits. No one but the girl behind me witnessed the oatmeal incident. One dumb tactile realignment, and one person snooting her nose up in disdain. And suddenly I'm walking around naked, called out like *The Invasion of the Body Snatchers*? Was it my paranoia inflicting self-imposed exile from the recognized in society? Was I responsible for the negative emotions being aimed at me? I hadn't done anything, really. Just perception, and what I alone knew about myself. Maybe no one would know if I really tried to stay in rank, but I couldn't hide from being branded as homeless, within and without. I didn't sign up for anything.

What was this witchcraft?

Instant social demotion.

No form to complete. No one to say yes, or no. I was fucking homeless. Still wearing what I wore at the house a few hours ago. But sure as shit outed, in a city with well-honed "dar." I couldn't hide. The poison radiance of an outcast. A second-class citizen. I've stumbled around plenty of times looking like total shit, coming off wasted and destitute. No one cared. The thought didn't occur to me.

But *snap!* All that anyone will learn about me from here on out will be that I'm homeless.

What was this witchcraft?

"Hello... Good morning. Police..."

You hear the cop's voice first through the blanket you have pulled up over your head. Then his flashlight beam undilates your eyes like an explorer peering through a wall of ice. You pull the blanket from your face, tucked beneath your chin like a child.

It's strange, like awakening inside a dream, to sit upright in dark morning half asleep, and realize you're in the middle of an empty Golden Gate Park, silent under the moonlight, a cop writing you a ticket. Did you pass out? Everyone bailed on you? Went back home? She's gonna be mad at you...

"Stay there, don't get up," the cop said. "You have any ID? Anything with your name on it?"

"Yes," I said. You wake up fast.

"Wow. One of the few."

I gathered my stuff, keeping the blanket over the beer.

"No, don't get up, you can stay down. Go back to sleep."

No one around.

"Sign here."

As I write this sentence on February 28, 2015, after thirteen months living homeless, my ticket count for sleeping in the park has exceeded 21 citations. I have four other unattended tickets for open container violations. I'll leave them all unattended to. None of the homeless respond to citations for "lifestyle violations." Police run my name every time they cite me, but with over a baker's dozen of outstanding warrants for failure to appear I'm left alone.

Any cop making a traffic stop in Cleveland or Dallas would drag your dear old grandma to jail if they spotted even one warrant.

Not the SFPD.

"I'm not going to show up, I can tell you that," said a cop on a cop dirt bike. He was citing me and another guy for open containers, the beers we were drinking. His ticketing required he appear in court as a witness to us winos.

"Well it was nice meeting you then," my drinking compadre told the cop.

I'd know the guy a few days, young black dude in a Niners cap. Every morning he showed up to Panhandle carrying a hot deli-baked chicken and once he had wrapped sushi. All stolen by running out of Whole Foods with a shopping basket of random items selected as diversions to the sought after prize. Store employees were only allowed to run so far before having to turn back, letting this guy go. We picked at the bird with our fingers.

"And can you two do me a favor and put the pot somewhere it can't be seen?" the officer asked us, tearing the second ticket from its book.

He handed me the bird catcher's ticket, not mine. I pointed this out as I traded the tickets.

Vrroom. vrroom.

I burned mine. He wiped his face and hands with his.

If only I'd known food was in such abundance when I first hit rock bottom.

That everything was in abundance.

Everything I Own
February 28, 2015

One pair of black Merrill shoes (left one split held with duct tape).

One biker-grade leather jacket.

Two pair of black jeans, worn one over the other.

One black T-shirt promoting The Spark Foundation.

One insulated hoodie embroidered "San Francisco" (meaning it's got that space-age warm insulation)

One pair of socks.

A Big River Outdoors sleeping bag (original one, just sewn together with visible stitches like Frankenstein's Monster).

Three spools of thread and a sewing needle.

One medical crutch.

A dark green 40-inch umbrella.

A pair of green wool knit gloves.

A small metal pot pipe with a screw-on lid, and a black Bic lighter.

A cell phone (no smart anything).

A laminated copy of a mock-up I made for this book so I can talk to people on Haight Street about it.

The two PC drives my Texas girlfriend said smelled like urine which she mailed back to me and are now in Jenny's closet where she protects them.

Other than this list, no comb, container, or doodad belonged to me except the acoustic guitar my daughter put stickers all over, and the Bulova watch passed down to me from my Great Grandfather which were both still in the loving hands of my friend in New York who I'll never forget said to me at about 12:04am on January 1, 2014, twice and

very seriously, at the end of a phone call I made to him wishing Happy New Year:
"You know you're insane, don't you?"

There is no such thing as a man-made necessity.

If a space traveler from some distant solar system walked up to you and asked "What planet is this?" and you replied "Well, this is Earth, but I'm homeless," the space traveler would probably gasp and sympathetically wonder, "What happened to your home planet?"

This space traveler – using a very literal translation device - would have no idea what you and I expect to be implied by the marginalizing term "homeless." If you had time to describe to the space traveler what you meant by using the word homeless, the traveler might politely say that the translator recommends the word "exile" as a better fit to your predicament.

The American Homeless Companion is steadfast in its position that there is no such thing as homelessness, and that the use of the term homeless as a derogation is not just ridiculous but also exasperatingly mean.

We are each indigenous Earthlings, all of us. We are each home.

You are home right now, where ever you are reading this. Sure, you have to be polite and move if you happen to be reading this while reclining in a crippled antique Victorian Balloon Back chair tossed to the curb and waiting to be destroyed by a Sunset Scavenger employee who for the second time has warned you to move. There is rarely a good excuse for annoying people wanting to complete a civilian job. That said, you're home as long as there is undisputed time to be there.

No man owns untended Earth. Earth is not a product.

If you believe that tending to land, growing food, and helping Earth do what it naturally does equates to your ownership of that land, then *The American Homeless Companion* urges you to exhaust all of your resources and direct them to tending to as much land as you possibly can afford. You will profit and your investment will wield great power by way of necessity. To the point of ownership, no one's going to make camp atop your budding peach orchid any faster than they are going to obey a No Trespassing sign posted in front of seven acres of idle, unstocked, untended and unsown grassland - An ignored swath of natural space that would benefit from habitation and its natural byproducts, if only temporarily. Listen land owner, you're not going to anger anyone by growing plants that create food and oxygen. The plants won't need to be told what to do.

Tree-hugger hatred and digressive arguments about market conflicts cascade from this line of free-form thinking. So you have to flush away cost, and dump the product mindset. Easier than you think.

If you're homeless, mind that many, if not most of your so-called problems will also arrive from an incorrect mind-set. Yours. One that whispers "everything that's homeless as criminal." One that surrenders you to the homeless stereotype like a self-inflicted wound. A mind-set too soft to serve as a foundation for dignity as a homeless character. New homeless arrivals can easily believe "Oh well, I'm homeless now, so have to go insane or I have to be a criminal. I must be, otherwise I wouldn't be homeless now. Yes, I'm homeless now. I have to go steal a shopping cart."

Just like a land owner acting on imagined property rights, fulfilling an expectation. Homeless try destitution on for size as if they believe they are expected to wear it. It a flip-of-the-swith mindset that has deep, institutionalized social prejudice colored all over it. You've been assigned this. Act the part. The parts being suppressed in people a badge of honor granting them at least one valid station in life they can defend.

Like the land owner, the homeless need to stop caring. The appear to have, but they care deeply. Being homeless is the only thing they have to care about, and that needs to stop. The homeless need to stop caring, all the way. Stop doing the work of their detractors.

But aren't I going to smell like shit as a homeless person? I'm fucking homeless! Aren't you listening? I can't afford an apartment! I have no place to live! No place to shower. Put on clean clothes. Wouldn't that drive you insane? Aren't I now supposed to stay out of places I used to go, because they think I'm broke and I won't get served? Stop calling my friends because they'll know what it is I want the second they hear my homeless voice? And how long am I supposed to be able to hide my homelessness from loved ones?

I overheard a twenty-something homeless guy who was looking for a cardboard box he lost outside the food bank say "I thought the only thing I'm supposed to lose out here is my mind." He was a young South American looking fellow with a happy, event-less smile who practised his tennis swing of the backpack-filled stage of Christ's Church while it seated and fed whoever wanted to show up each Saturday morning. He was a southpaw with a mean backhand.

Would you want your mother to hear you say that? Her little boy is anticipating, surrending to, losing his mind.

My God. She would weep. Her little boy.

The American Homeless Companion does not endorse the horrific and inhumane notion that losing one's mind, so to speak, is in any way automatic, necessary, fashionable or advisable upon entering homelessness, just as it would be rejected at any economic layer of society. Any argument about mental illness is a digression from the pure subject of Baseline Economics.

With no rules to homelessness, there are no fellow homeless to tell you what to do, what to be, or how to think. This is the freedom and the danger of homelessness as it currently exists. Tips in *The American Homeless Companion* such as Remember Which Drug You're on run directly home to the caveat of homelessness' unrelenting freedom, and the obligation its inhabitants have to their own self-control.

Remember this: Attitude is everything when you first arrive.

Your self-image at the point of entrance absolutely determines the quality and content of your experience. If you arrive to find peace, you do. If you arrive expecting war, you'll likely find one, or several, waged against you.

If you're angry and rude to people, you better love being that way and love the neglect you'll be awarded for it. Because at Baseline you are on you own. No one cares what your attitude is, or how tough or independent you are. That guy with the lawnmower over there doesn't care. Only you should.

If you think you'll change when you enter homelessness, you are dead wrong. If you fear your true self, you better think about that first part.

If you wonder whether or not you've completed your purpose in life, if you're still alive, you haven't.

You'll enter homelessness at the same time a small wave of other new social outcasts arrive, and you'll remember them, and watch them adjust. Each person unique, unusual and slightly banged out of character when you first meet. Know that how you feel upon entering homelessness is likely how you'll feel for quite some time, the first several weeks for certain, probably the first few months.

I arrived a wound-up bundle of frustration, daring the Universe to throw another stone. Daring anything else in life to go wrong so I could laugh, raise my fist, extend a middle finger, shout in victory: "Nice try! Nothing can hurt me now! What are you gonna do? Huh? Make me homeless or something?!"

It's fair to say that behind the confidence of my clenched fist was the luxury of legal identification and a pre-paid Millennium debit card issued from a check cashing company called The Money Store. The flimsy card without raised numbers was active with a $200 balance, and just waiting to be swiped at the front desk of any number of week-by-week residential hotels speckled across The City.

Had I hit hit homelessness flat broke knowing nothing but, "Hey I guess no one will be surprised now if I grab something out of this garbage can and eat it on the street," instead of having some money to watch melt away on pricey made-to-order sandwiches and 12-packs of Pabst Blue Ribbon from Whole Foods, then I'd have found myself putting up with the punishing schoolyard politics of food, drugs and relationships that newbie homeless tackle in the process of banding together with like minds. Very unpredictable. Little direction. No body comes to you. It's the other way around, unless you are a girl.

I got lucky.

Her name was Harriett Kilgore.

Her beagle, Queenie Bee, introduced the two of us. She ran up to where I sat beneath the 40-Ounce Wind Chimes and began licking my face. Harriett followed.

"Queenie Bee, leave him alone!"

I could tell by the way Harriett strode up the hill towards where I sat that we were a couple. Experience fires a flare. It was only a matter of what I would say first, which fortunately suffered 8-track grade wow and flutter as Queenie Bee lapped my lips. The dog's tongue tasted like Fritos when I tried to say, "This girl wouldn't harm a fly."

Queenie Bee, properly understood, is a vicious attack dog with a lineage bathed in blood. The bow-legged bitch went teeth-exposed for the right testicle of a polite kid asking for one of my Pabst, before Harriett even sat down next to me. I thanked the dog for that, because I wanted to be alone with Harriett.

Otherwise Queenie Bee attacks at whim. Strikes on unsignaled, hair-trigger instinct. Man, woman, dog, squirrel, organism, doesn't matter. At any moment, there's a dust-stirring ruthless assault and cries from Harriett to "Get your butt back here!"

Lumpy, the west park's toughest tough guy, didn't know his fellow homeless pals referred to him as Lumpy until a few somewhat heartless friends begged Lumpy to beat the shit out of someone called Lumpy. Lumpy also attacks at whim. So after beating himself up about that Queenie Bee up and carved the rear of Lumpy's right thigh like a plate of prime rib at the end of a Sunday buffet table. Harriett began looking for a box to contain her dog's corpse in, but fido lived to bark about it. Bit Lumpy during a period of person reflection.

Luck ran out. A week later the rude, tireless canine up and gnawed on a cop's craw which won the mutt jail time in a South San Francisco animal shelter, an incarceration which carried a tab that for several months indentured Harriett into the servitude of someone she never identified to me. Only that this person had a kid attending Harvard Medical. Harriett didn't ask me for the money because I was broke. If I had it I would have regretted giving it to her.

Like Hemingway described Maria in *For Whom the Bell Tolls*, Harriett walks like a colt. Her prance is as petite as it is powerful. An upward skip from both tiny feet I'd watch in the moonlight as I followed her across empty tennis courts leading to our camp in the thick brush behind the backboard. Harriett resembles a blonde Rosanna Arquette if the actress never had a dental plan.

She does not shave and has little hair to show for it. Homeless shed dozens of pounds during their first six months outside, so don't look for a drop of fat on Harriett's warm, slender build, which is as strong as two of me combined and pulls her six-wheeled carry-all contraption of clothes, blankets, dog food and weather-proofing with a posture of military discipline and deliberate intent best described as stateless pride on parade.

Harriett noticed in the morning if I threw the sandwich she prepared me for dinner over my shoulder instead of eating it like I said I would. When I complimented her on how delicious it was. You can't be polite to her. Just honest. She reminds you of how wasteful your life as a housed person was. How so much waste got generated trying to please other people, and not make waves.

Harriett goes with the flow, man. She doesn't get upset at the point of the story where after she gets all bundled up warm and perfect in her sleeping bag with Queenie Bee tucked inside, she suddenly, "inconveniently and of course then" has to pee. She says she farts too. Poor dog.

She whispers to me not to move beneath the tarp arched over her bike. Otherwise the rain that collects up there will drip to our noses. She reads David Wilke in bathroom candle light which she falls asleep to. She wonders aloud when you will touch her breasts which are tattooed with a pencil thin blue outline of an eagle spreading its wings.

Golden Gate Park had been Harriett's home for over 20 years when Queenie Bee introduced us. Harriett bore two healthy children while living in the park, and like folks my age, she'd undergone a few typical procedures and minor surgeries at California Pacific Medical Center and UCSF Medical. Harriett was a fully functional resident of San Francisco, didn't matter where she lived. Resembling an old hippy, Harriett naturally merged into the Bay Area scenery and did nothing to create prejudice against herself.

Harriett acted As If.

Loud when she had the right to be. Fit as a whistle. Cornbread sense of humor. Will tell you she "likes" you if she wants to have sex with you instead of using the word "love" because "I love everybody, you see?"

Harriett was a Baseliner before I knew what the word was. Her Summer of Love congeniality made Harriett known and welcome within any group, clan, tribe, or drug circle in Golden Gate Park. Entering homelessness was like opening a surprise present with Harriett along side. She made it a slowly appearing photograph in a tray of developer fluid – A once hidden world around you slowly exposing itself with a new layer of detail.

Harriett knew exactly how to set up camp, any camp, on soil or concrete, fast. She wouldn't flop and pass out. This little girl placed bedding, sheets and blankets carefully down. Set lighting, supplies, and dog-world up, organized knowing the night was mostly dark, when things disappear.

Harriett was a Master Class in Baseline Economics, but similar to Jack Kerouac, she just didn't know what to call it yet.

During days, Harriett, Queenie Bee and I would wag around The Horseshoe at the front of the park, telling family who quickly became very close friends of mine half-truths like: "Hey Ziggy, meet my husband! He likes to argue."

That hubby was me. I'd smile, admiring the colorful wool sweater Harriett wore knowing that, when my last wife bought it from The Territory Ahead during our second vacation to Santa Barbara, she never imagined it worn a few years later by a dancing hippy in a drum circle passing me a lit hash pipe.

You promise yourself after the first time your fuck up that if you ever offer a sandwich to family, you make the fucking sandwich for them. Don't let them touch anything. This isn't about cleanliness, it's about greed and theft. When a homeless person makes a sandwich, they prepare a vertically built container, bread bookends compacting all of the food and condiments you have.

"You should have been paying attention! That was all our food! We just got it!" Harriett yelled me awake. The moon was full and she woke hungry, wanting to toss together a snack beneath moonlight bright enough to read ingredients by.

Harriett cursed each missing item out loud as she rummaged deeper into the rolling basket attached to her bike which moments ago served as our headboard. She named each food product that was essentially stolen from us so I'd hear what we'd lost. The sliced ham in natural water, drained jar of sweet pickles, a block of government American cheese, the bread "except for these two crunched up ends!" Harriett grumbled. "We don't even have any napkins left!"

Yup. All long gone since Hippy Hill earlier in the evening. While Harriett danced in the drum circle and gallivanted around, I unknowingly watched our chow go bye-bye saying "sure" to any friend of Harriett's who walked up and asked "can I make one too?"

Only a week in, I didn't realize how starved family allowed themselves to become. I still didn't know how easy it was to eat. To get fresh, free food. So many homeless seemed to be clueless about this as well. Believe me, if all you want to do as a homeless person is eat - no drink, no drugs, no library card - you can eat world-class clean free food non-stop. Read on.

This morning, now a year homeless, I sat down to eat on door steps between Haight and Oak Street. Flat broke, it took me a mere 15 minutes on Haight to ask for and receive a warm, untouched 6-inch pork cheese steak, and then a pint of steaming Kung Pao Chicken, each handed to me by employees of some company who were served more food than they wanted to eat.

Taste that combination on your palette. Cheese steak. The cooked pineapple and rice. What restaurant has that combination on the menu, then charges you nothing? A Snapple All Natural Half 'n Half ($3 out the door) to wash it down with while reading my email on a $35 Samsung pay-per-minute internet-enabled cellphone.

A year ago, it was the sound of Harriett chewing on bread crusts sprinkled with aspartame. Telling me "turn that light off" as I use my cell phone to double check our basket for any food that was spared. Just one disappointment in a lightening round of naive disappointments I experienced in those early days. Disappointments in homelessness, and the homeless. I was brought up to believe it was human nature to share, and that sharing could be trusted amongst your closest circle of friends. I naively assumed this new group of friends would reliably monitor their sandwich portions, temper their condiment amounts, and leave Harriett and me, people they saw every day, with something other than nothing.

Wrong.

Homeless, nothing is what you end up with if you don't hold on to everything you desire to keep. Literally, attach it to you. Don't set you backpack down. It's theft will be labeled a "ground score" given up to finders-keepers rules. Even if the person who stole it is someone you peacefully interact with everyday, which 99% of the time is the case, if you take the time to get to know people. Homelessness is cleptoville, folks. Stealing from family tolerated so people who get ripped off can justify ripping things off to. If only to replace what they lost. More than twice I've been told I have someone's old backpack. Stuff rotates around. Disappears fast. Click! You just lost whatever you set down in the time it took to walk from the front of Club Deluxe to its street corner to shout at a fellow homeless chum how much you love them.

Your stuff is gone. Tough luck. Northern stole it, or maybe Jedi. You'd recognize them if supplied surveillance camera footage. But identification would add up to nothing. Police will tell you go dig another one out of a garbage can. That's the God's honest truth. Will say it through the window of the patrol car as they coast by, not stopping. If you were a dressed any other way than you are, cops would stop, asking for a description of your lost items. If you were harmed. Gone is best forgotten.

Let 'em steal, let 'em cut in line. Homeless don't

use manners, don't care what others get, certainly don't sample food for taste.

You'll never hear a homeless person say "excuse me, may I have a small spoonful of that to try first?"

The homeless don't starve beneath etiquette:

"Oh no, I'm fine, I'll be eating something a little later."

The homeless eat. Homeless ask to eat, or don't.

Our ill-mannered brothers and sisters on Hippy Hill did no wrong by helping to make all our food go away. They watched Harriett's new husband slap together a sandwich and dump mayo all over it and asked if they could make a sandwich too. I said yes and they made it their way. They made a fuckin' sandwich. A Dagwood. Gluttonous pig application of every consumable item available.

Status be warned. Homeless, your residual mannerisms will be ignored, cost you time and money, and could be observed as out of place by the suspicious. Displaying your thoughtful pedigree through politeness is an excellent idea around older homeless, and those equally demonstrative of patience and composure. However, left untempered, this naivete will leave you hungry more than once.

You'll curse yourself wondering why you hesitated to take a large portion – Why you didn't act like everyone else and take all you could?

I've seen Wiz the Wonder Junkie spoon up a first scoop out of a freshly opened peanut butter jar so lopping and huge that my mother would have grounded me for a month had I done the same in front of her. She would have grounded me on principal of her polite Southern upbringing in an impoverished home. Not because there wasn't enough peanut butter, it was all about looks and fear of other people's opinion of you.

The American Homeless Companion salutes The

Wiz for knowing and taking what he wanted. He was too much in the hunt for drugs of any kind to get his newly found dog licensed. His mom wouldn't send the money. Asked for it using my Facebook account. Mom's reply was come home and we'll make sure the dog gets legal. I could tell by her word choice that Wiz was missed and welcome back. Lucky Wiz for having Mom there. Foolish Wiz for preferring to spend the afternoon drinking a bottle of Robitussin cough syrup.

Homelessness is fertile ground for misinterpretation of how money works, how value is assigned and depreciated. A kid sits in front of the library on Page Street staring a Ronco-style multi-function coffee make, still in the box and wrapped because the plastic device with plastic cups probably makes coffee that tastes like plastic so the recipients sent it right to the trash. It is garbage. Industrial garbage spit out because it could be done. Make 1000, sell 10. We made a profit let's go home. Homeless are mostly under the illusion that everything has value and people wake up every morning excited to buy it.

"How much do you think I'll get this?" the kid asks a yuppie heading into the library.

"Who's going to buy it?" the yuppie smartly replies.

Why was it made. No, not those reasons.

Why?

Read on.

Harriett found a discarded sewing machine in such wonderful condition the owner still had the original box to throw it away in. Her plan was to hook it up to solar power so she could set up shop on Hippy Hill and generously "sew everyone's clothes back together."

It was a great idea. When you arrive at homelessness you're astonished by how many adults don't know how to sew as much as a button back on their clothes. So clothes take on a disposable character. Many homeless, including me, just replaced clothes instead of washing old ones, because like food, clothes are cheap and plentiful, mostly free.

Solar power sources are not. The cheapest 120 volt solar generator I could find was $500 on eBay. Harriett didn't want or need this news. Or an added 70 pounds to the weight she already hauled around. The idea fluttered away with the flapping of torn clothing.

Before March rain I bought Harriett a sorely needed new pair of boots with the last of my money. Hers flapped at the right heel and she told me "I haven't had a new pair of shoes in 20 years."

I had just arrived at a point of acceptance of being homeless, being with Harriett. It was not yet The Crossroads of Commitment for me. But it was a sunny Tuesday morning and Harriett and I had just finished breakfast on Haight Street. I didn't want her to have to beg, which I didn't know was called "scarping" yet, so I bought us blueberry pancakes which we ordered to go because of a no dogs allowed policy. Queenie Bee, not a service dog, ate most of our side of bacon.

Afterwards Harriett stretched her arms out wide and kissed me.

"So, I need a hundred dollars for new shoes and then I want to go down to the Panhandle and make lunch after I introduce you to Scott."

I had a hundred dollar bill, my last piece of paper currency. I handed it to Harriett who pointed out a pair of tough angle-high Refinery29 lace-up boots which matched her style and endurance requirements. But instead of those boots, while I waited outside, Harriett got talked into a pair of Wolverine Buccaneers dashed with a Jackson Pollack finish. They were not waterproof. The sales girl hadn't asked.

I walked in as the cashier wanted to know if Harriett needed her old pair of shoes placed in the new shoebox to take home with her. The cashier twisted the insides of each boot between her thumb and forefinger which animated the boots in a walking motion while she held an inquisitive look on her face. I laughed at this, which the cashier took as a cue to drop the eroded boots into a plastic waste basket below the register desk with a boom.

Harriett looked down at her new boots and clicked her heels like Ruby Slippers.

"I'll take that," I said, and the cashier handed me the change from the hundred, not Harriett.

This was not good.

I watched the heels of Harriett's new boots as she stormed away from me in anger. Mad enough to leave behind Queenie Bee and all of our belongings which I dragged as quickly as I could in Harriett's steaming wake. When I got close enough she began to hiss "that was so uncool. That was so, fucking, uncool."

I had it figured out by then, all out of breath. "Okay, sorry. I shouldn't have asked for the change..."

Harriett turned to me and screamed. "You know, you're not just going to go into that library every day while I do nothing but make sure we have food!"

This must have been building up. I saw myself as a pretty good provider.

Harriett's new boots fell apart in less than a month. No weatherproofing, and it rained hard until April Fool's Day. She thought I was being selfish when I hid in my waterproof sleeping bag clutching my laptop so sprinklers wouldn't soak it dead. She'd get up, get soaked tearing down camp, and march off with Queenie Bee. "Come on Queenie Bee, I'll take care of you in all this."

I wasn't turning out to be the husband Harriet had in mind. She dreamed aloud about that one.

"There's this guy up North, and I guess I'm kind of mad at him because he never came and swooped in and got me out of here like he promised he would," Harriett said.

She stopped, braced herself on her bike. Not sad exhausted. Not afraid to taste it. "Here I got you a beer with my last three dollars," she reanimated and said, digging into one of her backpacks. "You want a hat for your head?"

Keep your head warm, and your body will follow.

Each morning as Harriett and I strolled through the thick woods that dress the avenue side of the park we'd pass Roy, who was either on his way with his shopping cart to wherever he made his recycling rounds, or was sitting drinking Budweiser on the gold leaf tree.

Harriett and Roy didn't speak. When Harriett had nothing to say to, or about someone, well, there was history I didn't touch.

Word on the street from one unreliable person was that Roy was a bass player for a signed rock band I never got the name of, but was famous enough to be remembered by the person who didn't say it.

I never asked Roy about his rumored past as a rock star. When Haight Street Rusty told me how proud he was that a cousin of his was a musician in a band that sold records, I had since become a bit jaded by the routine falseness of the homeless. As much as I liked Rusty, and as much as he talked up Roy, I never saw the two together. I didn't question it because it didn't matter. The reality/fiction relationship I had with Rusty was five times as interesting and instructive as anything real, considering Rusty's limited life experience. A guy from nowhere with nothing personal to say about himself other than a projection of need and take. I remember the day Rusty realized how much he and I looked the same (that is if I shaved my beard). Same features. Like twins. He told me this after showing me how the bullet hole in his left thigh was healing. He was about right.

"Why'd some guy shoot you, man?"

"I don't know," Rusty replied in his low, growl voice which has a rough tone but a Gomer Pyle innocence.

"You don't know? Rusty what the fuck? Where? In front of McDonald's,"

"They have it on surveillance? They have the guy?"

"No, in the front of the park, by McDonald's. Where it begins to slope down?"

"Do you know him?

"No.

"And he just shot you."

"Three times."

"Fuck.

This type of vignette was the kind of story you always got from Rusty. A freeze frame in time with all it's context stripped away, so it's just this insane sounding turn of events, but what event only Rusty knows, or?

If Roy had been a rock star, he invested his money wisely. He carried with him a point-rendered ledger of five-figure sums he whispered pay dividends. I took a glance at the ledger of $20,000 to $70,000 figures stacked atop one another uncalculated while he totted with it one afternoon. Individual numbers, no recognizable arithmetic, account numbers or dates. Nonsense unless it yours.

The numbers scrawled in Roy's ledger were most likely bullshit. You see a lot of these kind of games played by older homeless and nutty younger ones. The pure attraction of numerical display, a fantasy of value.

Roy always had half a 12-pack of Bud stashed beneath the metal shopping cart he stole from Safeway before they replaced them all with plastic carts with locking wheels. Unlike all of the other recyclers I met in Golden Gate Park, Roy is the only one I know free of a methamphetamine addiction. Not to say Roy doesn't enjoy smoking speed when it's passed his way, or gladly pitching in a five dollar bill for it. Roy does. He just isn't bogged down in the dastardly speed cycle of earn-and-burn. He knows he has the choice to stop. A choice he passed on many years ago by accepting loss, so to speak. He takes his time, and only what he needs. Roy is Grade-A satisfied.

"Yeah, well peace and love and all that kind of stuff."

Roy likes to say that when his complexity meter begins to move.

Then he shuts up.

Roy and I have spent many hours together enjoying each others company on one of the few remaining public benches in Golden Gate Park.

The tucked away nature and classic simplicity of our one particular bench's over-painted green recline has been spared removal by the city thanks to its location deep inside a lightly-traveled Sleepy Hollow-like section of the park just below 6th Avenue.

Unless you want to sit on the ground, there are not enough places to be seated in Golden Gate Park. And forget the adjoining upper Haight, which has no outside seating at all, except for two: A really stuffy micro-brew, *The Magnolia Cafe.* And a really stuffy grocery store pipering people with AAA credit ratings boringly called *Haight Street Market.* Get 'em boys.

Sitting on a park bench, Roy the Recycler is a frightening iconoclast, the default image of a desperate, disgusting homeless person. He's the disturbing, disheveled *Aqualung* character which the British band Jethro Tull sings about on their album by the same name, sans the "eyeing little girls with bad intent" part of the classic rock song's misinterpreted libretto. It's strange to hear KFOG cue *Aqualung* up when you're sitting next to Roy, who is one of the few homeless left who listens to terrestrial radio through a thing with an antenna, you know.

In my first four months homeless, I watched three public benches like the one Roy and I often sat on disappear from Haight Street between Masonic and The Horse Shoe. The last one I saw get ripped out from its bolts faced the Western most corner of Haight and Masonic (*The Magnolia Cafe*, oops, down to one). That bench had become a Drinking Bird perch for three drunks who slowly tipped with every sip of their warm, shared Hurricane Malt Liquor until they'd slag into collapse on one another's' wrinkled shoulders. Max, Mama Bird, and Andy. Each, cheap screw-top wine bottles one day's sunlight away from spoiling to vinegar. Magnolia management got tired of white-boarding for their wait staff the proper way to explain to customers what a Drinking Bird was without chagrin, so the city plowed the bench into rubble with a backhoe that just happened to be on location in front of the micro-brew, there to uncover a gas line.

It needed to happen. Abuse of the bench had become blind. Diners at *Magnolia* seated in tables against the front window had about 15 feet away from them a row of homeless people shoulder to shoulder sitting on the top of the 30 foot long bench, feet up on the seats, all holding a cardboard sign scribbled with a tired pitch for money or food or "anything helps just need $15 for Seattle God bless" or "smoke me out." All staring at you eat, just like that, no shit. A convenient mall making it easy for you to select your chosen homeless donation, or maybe two, or all of us? They're rich, right? "I remember Rebound saying how they spanged $60 and a whole pizza for all of us from this techy. Stayed to ask if they needed anything else."

"Uh, yeah..."

"You have to get up, you fucking idiot!" I yelled at Max on Christmas Day as he laid flat out on his back on the sidewalk waiting for a chalk outline. He was dead out. It was just before noon. I was sitting on the soon-to-be-dozed bench in front of *Magnolia* and its freaking Christmas morning and here is this dead old man's body a few feet away from me on the cement. The scene made Roy the Recycler's behavioral abandon come off like Sir Richard Branson's palace etiquette. Max pissed himself, still out. Urine trickling away from his eroded mechanics' slacks. People stepping over him. How do you sit in the vicinity of this and ask a stranger for money or food unless you're using Dead Max as a prop to shake down people by targeting their sympathy. If a girl doesn't get mad at me for saying to a stranger "can you help me and my wife get a little something to eat? We're so sorry to ask," I'll give her two bucks if the tip we get is a ten spot. It's pimping. And when done with no negotiation its incredibly satisfying to both the pimp and the prostitute. I have added to hurl with a pitch for money (a wife, a dog, cat), and she does nothing but stand there. Lady give me $10, in the same motion I put $2 in her hand and poof!, I'm a Daddy.

I wanted nothing to do with Max. Any of them. They were homeless, but not street people homeless, not park life. They were squash faced, booze laced, sunken eyed, chin dropped nasty American bums. You wouldn't find Max or Mama Bird in the park. Andy had his own ambulance that carted him off to Dignity Health every other week. One Friday evening Andy went into convulsions in front of Fred's Market on Haight Street, flapping around on his side until he rubbed the skin off his elbows. I stood by the gurney as they loaded him into the back of the ambulance. Twenty minutes later, he appeared again on Haight Street.

"What happened?" I asked. "You Okay? They let you go?"

"Nah, just walked out," he hissed, eyes all squinty, bobbing right to left on his heels. "Piled up in the emergency room."

His hospital bracelet was still fastened.

Knocked out every day by 11am, it was just too goddamn depressing to have to look at these three dissolve themselves with alcohol. Local businesses blamed them for spooking tourists away from their clothing racks (forget about how the poisoned first impressions). Commuters snooted at them. Locals held their noses. Bad lessons were taught to newbies homeless with fledgling drinking problems.

Slouching on that bench in sight of the 43 Masonic MUNI stop, which caters to nearly 13,000 passengers a day who might be on their way to work and trying to look happy. Or passengers who paid nearly $10,000 to travel their family to San Francisco to see the positive sights the city takes credit for. Positive sights. Not someone who wants you to feel sorry for them.

A drunk, swaying Max pulling a long sheet filled with dirty clothes that resembles a colostomy bag is the reason Santa Hats should be illegal outside the North Pole. Mama Bird is undeserving her beautiful name, a name that should be celebrated, not blackened in an ankle-length polyester trench coat, in black sunglasses beneath a black leather bucket hat someone in San Francisco threw away. Mama Bird frightens children. I retreat from her invitation for a kiss. No way do I want to be thought of as a couple.

I tell Roy, all hot and bothered from going off about Mama Bird and the old drunk she passes out next to: "This guy Andy makes me want to throw up. I mean it, Roy. He's pickled. The kid is half our age and, I don't know."

I've never seen Roy drunk, which isn't saying much other than Roy can hold his liquor.

Most people who come upon Roy and his shopping cart in the back woods of Golden Gate Park turn and walk the other way, the same way they do Mama Bird. Roy doesn't give a good goddamn. In fact, it's hard to find a way to find less of a goddamn than Roy gives, either for his clothing or his appearance. Just take all the water-spotted cardboard cut-out-doll clothes, stir fry them quickly in light oil, then drop them on Roy. Hats, socks, boots, jackets. Doesn't even matter if clothes fall cardboard-side up. They suit Roy just fine. There's Roy all dressed to go. Still having a problem picturing Roy? Just Google "Aqualung." The album was released May 3, 1971. Look at the cover art.

No one asks Roy why he doesn't line up for a social worker to situate him into a single room with a sink and a monthly check for around $1,100. Unlike Harriett, people look at Roy and figure he doesn't need it. And they are right. Roy is well aware that he inhabits the deep end of homelessness, well aware that his appearance wakes many up at night in the cold sweat of a job-related nightmare. Roy shops at Safeway. It's a laugh. Leaves his cart outside unlocked and gets a shopping basket. He parts the clouds, no looking at the dozens of eyes trained on him from all directions. He shops, pays. "Yeah, well peace and love and all that kind of stuff."

Roy shares Harriett's math when it comes to state assistance.

"Well, you can let them put you up in some hotel for the rest of your life in the Tenderloin, then after you pay for that you can hope you can get filled up for the day at Saint Anthony's or First Unitarian."

A case worker hands you a key to a 10x12 room in the Kean Hotel and leaves for the rest of your life if you don't ask for anything else. No rent or utilities. You never have to speak to, or even meet, the management. You are free for life. No improvement in job prospects. Maybe $1,100 a month from the state is you add on that you are mentally ill. Welfare won't argue with you is you say you think you're a little bit insane. The state encourages the admission. Confession better expedites the process of moving certain people along a different track of state and federal assistance. A separate set of books in the poverty welfare industrial complex.

Garnishment for rent leaves you with around $300 a month to live on, which is why Roy puts the emphasis on getting your tummy to feel full at that once-a-day only Glide Memorial Church meal.

"I'm just not that kind of guy, don't you think?" Roy asked me.

Roy takes care of himself outside. "I don't need much. Don't ask for it. I may grab a leftover here and there and thank you."

Roy admits he's lost count of the number of times he's been ticketed by police for sleeping in the park. I've heard the number 70 from him. He once recalled 200. Either number is far from uncommon for current homeless who, after understanding the meaninglessness of the ticket, sleep through the citation process in protest.

I laughed one morning right in the cop's face as I watched him try and hand a ticket to Crazy Dave, who was cozy in a sleeping bag and boldly uninterested in being part of the Keystone Cop episode we were enduring after sleeping too late in Buena Vista Park. The night before, someone had given Chara - a homeless jewel electrifying enough to stroll a fashion runway in Paris - four 2-inch thick T-bone steaks still wrapped in butcher paper. Chara, who rarely speaks and when she does gives out only a mumble-giggle, gave the prime cuts of beef to me. Crazy Dave and I were the elders of Buena Vista park at the time, a camp-congested hill overlooking lower Haight. Marinated in Wish-Bone Italian Salad Dressing the steaks finished medium-rare along-side two russet potatoes wrapped in aluminum foil. We went out like fed lions an overslept past motorcycle cop time.

"Are you really going to sit there and smoke that while I'm standing right here writing your friend a ticket?" the cop asked me as he laid Crazy Dave's ticket on top of his closed sleeping bag. As he left it there, Dave reached his arm out towards me wanting the Four Loco I was drinking.

"Dave, hang on. We just need one open container violation this morning, not two."

I handed him the beer so I could sign my ticket. The can disappeared inside Dave's sleeping bag. It could be tracked by a muffled slurping sound.

"You mind if I keep this pen?" I asked the officer. "These things are like gold out here."

He let me keep his pen.

"Is that really a social security number for Miami?" the cop asked. I did not have a driver's license. Homeless person stole it.

"Yup. Sure is. All the low numbers go to the East coast. My daughter was born in Manhattan so hers begins with a one."

You know my ticket count.

Crazy Dave after 10 years in the park: "Lost count."

Roy the Recycler after two decades in the park and God knows how many forgotten: "Yeah, I got enough to send me to San Quentin. So peace out and love and all that stuff."

So If this racking up of tickets written by badges not only unashamed to tell you they won't be appearing at your court date as your accuser, but who also consistently empower themselves by telling you they'll let slide ("this time") the six active warrants for your arrest which have added up since you burned each of them, sounds anywhere near liberatingly lawless, it is not.

Tickets peeled off for homeless sleeping in the park pile up in a sinister manner.

"Notice to appear" is printed in red above each traffic citation issued by the SFPD to the homeless. Cops would like to have your ID to help fill out the ticket but they also happily accept "my wallet got stolen" and any fake name you can match a signature to. Some ticket books

I've been cited from actually have a box to check with the words "No ID" next to it. Imagine that. A notice to appear in court issued to a person who presents no ID. Wonder when that person is going to show up?

The net of this pile up of unprosecuted tickets is extra ammo for the District Attorney. Closets stuffed with dry power. Tickets still awaiting resolution that any D.A. in George Gascon's district would instantly prosecute, rounding up all fugitives in an overnight dragnet. But the SFPD just waits to introduce and slide over a few active warrants when it pleases them, say, to increase the weight of a new charge. Oh, and this person has six other outstanding warrants as well as failures to appear, your honor.

Just here to pick up your stuff after San Francisco Public Works stole it all from where you've called home for six months? Well, now it seems these tickets you've piled up have come home to roost.

I scream at Roy: "San Francisco lets these slide like we are all going to just disappear. Let them slide until they decide they can use them to their advantage. But until then, they just coil up. They lay there, like snakes in the summer grass."

"Yeah, so peace out and love and all that sorta stuff."

Roy has never had to face a decision by a D.A. to slide a few of his millions of "traffic tickets" to the blind side of guilty justice because Roy shares Harriett's passion for avoiding rehabilitation, as well as cops. Roy's disinterest in having anything more in the world than what fits in his shopping cart goes a long way towards obscurity too. The grief, escape, mischief, pioneering, intoxication and spite of homeless company carries no price tag or penalty. No trail etched by the observations of others. You can disappear, or hide in plain sight.

"It's really impossible to tell the difference between our homeless and housed congregation," Reverend Ryan confesses from his pulpit at Christ's Church, a ministry that secretly enlists select homeless, like Harriett, to help operate and secure its location north of the Park.

His worship holds a key here for all to strongly consider. Ninety percent of the prejudice and distrust and resentment dealt to the homeless would vanish if homeless people would simply dress better. Act like they are on this side of the garbage dump. This country hemorrhages used clothes and there is a cornucopia of food nationwide. The tools are there if you want to fit in. Leaving no excuse for feeling outcast. The blame squarely on the poorly dressed ones. And don't get me wrong, in San Francisco you can wear clothes that look like they went through Eli Whitney's original cotton gin, twice, and still come off looking fashing-forward if the clothes are clean and radiate a sense of purpose. You know the difference.

Forget psychologists and bridge programs and counseling and even housing as homeless remedies. Just look normal for crying out loud! Is it a sin to say those words? Are we violating some weapons-grade politically correct liberal non-profit-minded hands-off rule by pointing out that yes, there is a normal in this country? Turn on the TV. Look. Normal.

I didn't eat from garbage cans, beg for cigarettes, wear ripped clothing, hang my head down. I ate from warm to-go containers of the city's finest food blessed by generous, partying people. I walked into and purchased from any business I wanted to. I made myself accepted. No one was waiting for anything from me. What was there to be so damn upset about?

My seemingly effortless transformation into a closeted homeless person fueled my animosity towards those in my arriving class whose claws you could still hear scraping against the wood surface of homes they refused to admit they no longer had.

I marveled at the surrender to stereotype displayed by Don the Traveler. Don hauled around five pieces of matching luggage neatly packed on two roller boards, with a bag slung over his shoulder. But he never changed clothes. Same dark gray suit matching the luggage. Not a scuff, on anything. He has a tidy droop like a fat old train conductor, less the engineer cap with the one ticket. I've never seen Don read anything or carry on a conversation next to someone other than me. He shows up for breakfast at Glide, then walks 35 blocks to the Panhandle and lays down on a bench like he's stranded in an airport. Every day. I have no idea what he might have in all that luggage. I waited three months before I spoke to him.

"Hey Don, what's with all the luggage? When's the livery car coming to pick you up?"

"Oh, I won't be here long."

That was last month. I was told that last year.

I still wonder.

Don's just the opening act for The Mover and The Racer, who each sleep on the taped vinyl front seats of their rusting Detroit pickup trucks. Two car dwellers obeying nothing but registration and alternate side parking. Both too stubborn to accept their time has past, they are out of the workforce, what they pack rat in their pickup beds are artifacts from another time, gone never to return. All their efforts go to resuscitating the past, a dead body that has not yet hit the floor. Trying to sell old stuff from an old residence using old knowledge they gained at an old job back in the old days which makes old stuff valuable the old fashion way in this old racing jacket I never take off and the old stories I always tell in the old way of acting clueless so you could strike up a good old conversation about nothing.

The Mover and The Racer spend their San Francisco afternoons patching torn tarps stretched over their mountain ranges of possessions protected beneath burlap, cardboard and bungee cords. Taking a sign from beneath a wiper that reads "you can move your truck now." A flat-assed truck packed with scuffed furniture. Five-gallon buckets. Something metal. Something coiled. Something important to someone else. A promise to dead loved ones to protect something plastic and worthless to the outer worldly. In other words, shit. That never gets used. Replaceable in hours. Just kept. The meaninglessness strains the mind. But there's a reason. Read on.

Oh wait, these two guys have cars. They can drive away. Why don't they?

The Mover and The Racer yield the stage to an even darker display of homeless limbo. People holding onto to the past, but reaching for it like parts the cannot see or organize. Their world empty of anything solid, any real person, any logical progression. The world has becomes a haunted house to them. They cower in solitude, fear or self-pity. Become tragic. Pop-culture cartoons wearing frowns, impossible to trust (the word was not "help") and depressing to communicate with.

Meet the Grade School Teacher. Wearing a full length dark gray wool overcoat and jet black Jackie O sunglasses, The Grade School Teacher prefers to lurk with her back pressed against the shelves in the Audio Books & Large Print section of the library. Her greyish black shoulder length hair flared out like Phil Spector's courthouse wig.

She recognizes me from the food bank. Sits down next to me, still wearing her weird glasses, not turning her head. I smile so her peripheral vision picks up that she is recognized and loved. I get no response. She answers her cell phone like a nightmare.

"Hello?" she says vacantly into a flip phone, which

did in fact ring so there are batteries in it even though there's no one speaking on the other end.

"Who is this?" she says without anger. "I don't know you."

Now you are interested and listen. She's reading cue cards written by Rod Sterling. "I'm not sure. Do I know you? Why that? No one will give me a place to live yet."

The Grade School Teacher was accused of improperly touching a child, so a judge properly ruined her teaching career. She did the rest.

"I'm innocent I never touched anyone and they didn't believe me I lost everything and no one will call me back and I have speed dial," she said without punctuation so I doubt she taught language skills.

I buy her story. She doesn't strike me as the child fondling type. She's too weird for that. Show me a basement collection of mummified cats and yeah I'd assign her that. The Grade School Teacher is easily taken to the edge by the unpredictable. She has a fit if you rub up against any part of her body. A minor shoe bump as you reach past her for the coffee creamer in the breakfast line sends banished educator into hysterical choruses - what she probably should have been screaming back in class before the dogs were spoken to and unleashed: "Don't touch me! Don't get near me! Don't touch any part of my body! If you touch me again I'm going to delete your name from my phone!"

Harriett holds the record in my category of Most Sane Homeless Woman. I fell in love with Harriett very quickly because of that. She liked me to understand her thinking about matters, which assured me there was thinking going on. I thought I understood her. And I thought I understood, or at least had a reason for, letting her go. Homelessness was so free. I thought she was a burden. Her presence attracted more cops than I was used to, so I got less sleep (notice how concerned about ticket's

I'd become). A dog steals away as much happiness at it gives. I wasn't in an environment that fostered long-term thinking. I still miss the dickens out of her.

The removal from time and calendaring you experience well into homelessness brings a totally new experience to breaking up. I began trying to ditch Harriett whenever we became far enough away from one another. I hated going to her AA meetings, her tendency to blow $7.50 on a "Chicken Bowl!" no bigger, or taller, than the original iPad, the way she awarded a church, not me, the production responsibility for her CD of acoustic numbers which ended up sounding like a motivational cassette you play driving from Salt Lake City to Lubbock, background hiss and all.

One morning it became the third of four days she wasn't around and that was it. No thought about anything else, and yes, relief, temporary.

Then here's the difference being homeless. I run into her, probably that day, sitting with a few other family I know and one I don't. I sit and Harriett keeps talking. She handed me her guitar and that's when I got her CD too, hand-drawn cover, unprinted disc. I declined the axe, just happy to see every one. Really warm about Harriett, and it's cool, Fall coming. No mention of our fling, except somewhere within many topics when Harriett says "yea, it was short and sweet."

This is great. In, out. All is one forward motion into improvement and experience. In days she's just Harriett again. I lose access to the little girl.

Harriett would have been number one in line for free housing and living expenses had she given a damn about being part of the process. Harriett harbored no illusions about the trials and inhumanities of re-admittance into the land of the housed.

"I don't see myself as that kind of person. Living in

the Tenderloin. Hearing from a social worker."

This was one night when Harriett and I relaxed in a camp she uncovered overlooking the Conservatory of Flowers. We dined on four pork chops smothered in BBQ sauce and blackened on a $6.00 disposable aluminum grill, a quart of Safeway Deli Fresh Macaroni Salad, foil-wrapped corn on the cob seasoned with butter and Morton's Celery Salt, and three quarts of Hurricane Malt Liquor. Our view of the flowers was unobstructed, and we were completely hidden. Add cement, and where we relaxed would have been a $9,000 a month studio. Our cost, Zippo.

"I don't think I'd fit in. Or want to," she said. "Going through that process. Section 8 housing vouchers and that. Living in that condition. It's not me, don't you think?"

Now. Find a garage overhang that doesn't bear a no-trespassing sign. Here's a shelter when it rains. Absence of a no-trespassing sign is a clue that the owners are Baseliner friendly or Baseline indifferent. Introduce yourself. Be nice and say thank you - if they deserve it - and no matter what clean up your crap. Next time it rains they may offer you a shower if you converse with them as the same person every day. Remember that you're no longer working all alone to survive. Natural Providership has kicked in and you're trucking your way towards Dense Now. Your body learns to pick up and save adult pairs of shoes left to gather, regardless of their temporary weight or that conversation you're deeply involved in with Mountain, who suggests you buy pot from him and not so much from everyone else. Since Baseliner's burn through shoes, having them to offer ensures love, food, pot, jewelry and who knows.

What if they fit perfectly, Cinderella?

"I think guys get taken care of better than us."
- Harriett Kilgore

Fox Sports soccer commentator Charles Wollin will walk past the darkened garage port your sleeping bag is tucked into, stop, and take an interest in you, first asking if you are hungry.

Of course you say "yes" and he instructs you not to go anywhere as he takes off to "go grab a beer with a friend."

About 45-minutes later he returns with a bag for you which contain a jar of Planters salted peanuts (a six dollar item, yeah), a Cliff Bar, a chicken wrap, and a bottle of Glacier Smart Water "because it's got a lot of electrolytes in. What was your name again?"

Charles wants to know how you became homeless, and wants to "help with food or anything I can." You cautiously tell him how you have some money coming in soon, and a plan to boot.

Harriett is beneath her sleeping bag beside you. "Charles, thanks a lot," you say. "This is above and beyond the call of duty."

"At least you have a plan, that is so positive and what I always say is 'chin up', you know what I mean? Chin up?" Charles repeats.

You raise your chin for him. He says "I want you to keep me informed of your progress, and I'll be happy to help and buy you food. That's a pen there you have isn't it.

Write down my email address. It's Charles, my name, Wollin at Gmail."

You ask him if there is a "dot" between his first and last name in the Gmail address and Charles' eyes widen in amazement and he looks you up and down like you're a specimen.

"Boy, you are sharp. We have got to get you out of here."

You jot down Charles' Gmail address as he chatters "do you have a cell phone?"

"And when the check comes you're just going to deposit it, right?" he wonders. "What account do you have? With Chase? Wells Fargo?"

"Thank you again Charles," you say making sure he sees you have his Gmail address. I'll keep in touch and thank you so much for the food."

He's happy and leaves and Harriett sticks her head out and reaches for some peanuts from the jar which you open against a vacuum-packed suck.

"I've noticed guys get more help from homie's than girls do," she observes

Harriett is correct in her confusion. It does not compute.

"Never Feel Sorry for Yourself, That's The True Measure of a Man."

My grandmother we lovingly called Gammie.

She outlived her husband and her two grown children, and all of her nine brothers and sisters. Gammie is the happiest person I've ever known. She means too much for me to use the word "was."

There are three sayings that have held me together through life. Sayings I've repeated in my head in governance of my decision making. All three were told to me first by Gammie. All three in sync with a lesson.

"Haste makes waste."

"Sticks and stones may break my bones but words will never hurt me."

And the chief important lesson among all, immeasurable in its empowerment:

"Never feel sorry for yourself, Danny. That's the true measure of a man."

Gammie heard my voice growing younger in my 40s. She never said that, I just put it together from calls that decade when she would greet my voice with "Danny, you sound like a little boy!"

Near the age of 100, before my little sister called me with the news that our Gammie had died, Gammie gave me more magnificent jewels of wisdom than most around her expected she had forgotten.

Of all the things Gammie gave me other than my

mom, one truth, one dynamically all-purpose instruction has replaced an unknown number of silly, regrettable, expensive and dangerous pieces of guidance which do close to what it does, alone.

In an early email I describe myself to my friend Jane Weedman who was an English professor of my childhood, managed a punk rock band I played in called *The Tone,* lived with me in New York for a few months after my wife split, and lives in a garage-sized gingerbread house on Cloud Top Road in Canyon Lake, Texas with a broken down nut named Dale who Jane says "he's jealous of you" and prevents me from calling.

"Don't call," Jane writes. "I know you're there."

"Jane. I woke up when the car parked next to where I slept on the sidewalk started up for work at about 6am, so my sleeping bag was exposed to traffic going by. A cop would pass by soon, maybe stop. I got up, always in pain, and rolled up the sleeping bag sitting next to the apartment building I slept in front of. It was freezing and today was the first weekday I was out of money.

I normally get hot water for 50 cents and mix instant coffee I bought using the food stamps but not this morning so I was terribly cold as I walked to the Panhandle restroom but the men's room was out of order so thank God I didn't drink coffee before walking there.

I tried to stay warm by eating some bagels I had but was getting mad about everything. I always feel down in the morning, and sorry for myself which is a big no-no and I should have just made cold coffee for the positive energy but I got madder and threw the bagels, hurting my arm, then there was a basket of free apples that appeared which I grabbed.

Ate only one, leaving the rest. I became so angry I

started to cry and scream, and I knew I was throwing food which I should not do but I got rid of an entire carry bag of food from the food bank, so I lost my pillow too."

No matter what your attitude when you arrive at Baseline, it is easy to occasionally feel sorry for yourself during your freshman excursion. Easy to feel sorry for yourself because the things that tend to frustrate you early on are the basic things you took for granted. These are also the basic things you learned during childhood, and have never had to go without the supplies for since.

"You forgot to brush your teeth."

"I would have remembered if I had a mirror to see myself in, or a bathroom sink."

A shirt tag left out. Mom fixed that with a careful tug on your neck so kids wouldn't laugh at school.

Your fingernails. Noticing your left thumb nail get dirt under it and break. The nail is going to fall off. It doesn't hurt and it won't.

It hurts to see a piece of you get hurt. You cared for it, the way you were taught by your Dad who let you use his nail clippers after you asked him what he was doing.

To face the fact that it doesn't matter anymore breaks a cherished contract with your family, who loved every part of you. Even your little nails.

Suddenly something becomes most important of all. The most important stuff, you think. Not the stuff you wanted to run out the door and do. The stuff you left at home.

You are often alone during moments of self-pity, when you feel your innocence return. When you once again feel like merely a child, like remembering not to scratch the skin off an itchy mosquito bite because your shirt is dirty and there's no cortisone cream. Homeless, these moments and the memories of their genesis become even lonelier when you let yourself start missing a bathroom cabinet you can stare into, trying to remember what cortisone cream looks like.

Feeling sorry for yourself wells up from your earliest memories, uncluttered by brand names and people and life. Feeling sorry for yourself is a powerful urge early on in homelessness. You realize you're just this little child who had to learn little things. Your sorrow is for not staying that way. A shoe lace that breaks on a cold morning when your 50 year-old fingers are freezing reminds you of the relative who taught you how to tie your shoes when you were five and was so proud of you.

Proud of everything you were going to grow up to be and were destined to accomplish.

Self-pity feeds on this flavor of sorrowful reflection.

You must overcome this.

Never feel sorry for yourself, it's the true measure of a man.

One night beneath my sleeping bag I heard an approach and saw a light shine through, expecting to hear a cop say "people are calling" which is always a lie.

What I saw instead was the smiling face of James Cromwell look-alike Scott Free, holding out a paper plate in his generous hands with the offer "hot food?

Those were the first words I ever heard Scott Free say.

A former building inspector, he dated Harriett before I showed up. Harriett had no fond words for the seven footer in permanent Woolrich Irish. But she could deconstruct Scott Free's Urban Coffin with more dramatic build than Marisa Tomei can describe a Limited Slip Rear End.

"Check it out. He could be in there sleeping right

now," Harriett said, pointing out what I thought was a row of four-foot high compost bins covered in a light brown sheet.

What it was happened to be a bed in a box. A small dwelling in a box, really. Coffin-like in shape, size and creepy shroud, Scott Free's rolling shelter was a wire and wicker-tied pile of mixed metal, cardboard and plastic do-dads and aluminum real estate yard signs.

The coffin is soft-walled, so it's not as heavy as it looks, neatly covered with brown waterproof tarp and a matching hotel bed sheet. Foam padding plugged open gaps to fight draft. For easy theft, Scott's Urban Coffin was riddled with makeshift drawers and kitchen containers holding things like Scott's clothes, a slew of useful tools he happily loaned (if they weren't stolen), cooking and eating utensils, an acetylene torch and an upside-down steel bike basket that together formed a hot stove. On cold night, central heat from two internal candles. To keep from getting up, a piss jar and rubber tube. Scott empties the catheter bag (a gallon milk jug) on the grass of the Panhandle across the street. He's polite enough not to let his corner of homelessness, someone's three story house, smell like a 40-ounce through a human filter.

What Scott has cobbled together demonstrates a new urban school of Dazzle Camouflage, a short lived art practised on U.S. warships during the war in the Pacific. You don't believe or understand what you see, so you replace it with background. It works if you don't mind looking silly to the focused eye.

For Scott it worked like a motorcycle cover, or construction tools so heavy you can't walk away with. The workers took a safety break and left behind all this finger-pinching, toe-crushing gear you're not going to touch. Scott says he's never been disturbed while inside the crash coffin. Peace to sleep, jack off, roll freely. Scott's place in San Francisco. Towed by a bike.

A non-stop builder, Scott says he's never gone without material that he really needed. It magically arrives at the moment it's needed.

"All you need is right in front of you," he told me. "If you don't make yourself comfortable out here, you are crazy."

What's needed to do the job. Any job. Simply appearing. Always.

Scott didn't have a word for this phenomenon.

I would. Read on.

A homeless McMansion builder, Scott strung up a dwelling that resembled an igloo-sized hornet's nest fixed to the lower floors of the house's right face. In three days the no-rent abode had an adorable everything. Running water and electric lighting, a small sofa, TV and a George Foreman Grill Master missing its handles.

I warn him but Scott insists on building these backyard forts just to get ripped off every other day. Robbed by "friends" who'll say nothing and grin coasting past on a stolen bike as Scott accuses them of stealing his peanut butter and a fish scalar.

Scott will discover a break in (there is no door) then run around the surrounding blocks huffing after anyone who looks like they robbed him. Then he tires out and forgets it, asks Fred's Deli to front him a Steel Reserve, and goes to reassembling and replacing. Always a revision.

The homeless population can quickly spike around Scott's residence because its size and brashness begs the question bother us or leave us alone. As many as a dozen homeless will huddle around Scott's erector set in sleeping bags, one man tents, and blankets. The scene takes on a critical mass people find security in. So established was this dwelling that mail began getting delivered there. Scott used to get his mail across the street, an apartment complex he rented a room in for about 7 years. It's like he refused to leave, or at least go far. He continues to store his acoustic guitar in the car port of the apartment which he knows how to key into.

“They look at it like if they are going to have a homeless person living downstairs at least they have one they know,” he reasoned.

Less like the park, there are things to do at night when you sleep on the street, on sidewalks, doorways. There is night life, music, drugs, and a relative cease-fire between those who sleep inside and those who don't.

Scott Free cooks a hot plate over a propane torch secured by C-clamps and hands out plates of food. Nocturnal conversation and ease. San Francisco ghosts come out. Lots of drugs. The Tweekers have been fed, and now roam on bikes testing door handles like high fives and staring into drivers' seats. The subject matter is always seedy. Homeless woman surface in number and open up with conversation. Topics all about drugs, police, how bad or good the places they've been incarcerated are.

"Forget Sunnyvale. They kept me locked up for three weeks for standing kid with in front of an In-and-Out Burger. Never going back."

Occasionally a story.

"You rode to the Atlantic Ocean from Oklahoma City on a horse..."

"To Atlanta, and my dog here followed along," a kid told me one night, his girl and dog in front of Scott's with me. "His name's Button."

"Just you three? No one with you, no pickup truck following?"

"Na we just rode East, along side the highway."

"There had to been cops."

"Oh yeah. Go stopped once and asked where I'm going and I pointed and said 'East,'" he said, smiling, pointing East. :"'All the way?' they asked me and I said yep. That was it. They didn't ask me for ID or nothing."

His girlfriend grinned.

"The horse lived?"

"She's dead now, God love her. But she made it all the way. Fed her oatmeal and people would give us feed when we rode through their town. I got on TV once. News called me the High Plains Drifter."

His girlfriend laughed.

Riding through woods they turned a corner and a 7-foot bear crawling out of the brush.

"Button jumped on it and bit into the back of its leg, spinning around trying to shake Button off but he crunched down for dear life."

The bear ran away howling in pain. A chunk of its hairy leg in Button's jaws.

Lucky bastards.

Scott Free stirs Hamburger Helper over a make-shift military grade flame thrower duct-taped to a bike's handle bar basket. He pulls the skillet back and unscrews a nob on the face of the hobbie stove and flame shoots into the night sky the length of a telephone pole.

"Imagine if I pointed this thing at someone," Scott fantasized, smiling Irish and exposing his dental work fit for a skeleton.

"Hot food?"

Your trash. You just got it the way you liked it.

His name is Bill and he introduces himself as Bill but I've called him Priest since I met him in June. Baseline Economics was dawning on me. I sat one morning across from the tennis courts when Bill strolled by with his grocery cart. I recognized him because he circled with Harriett when he first arrived. About the time she and I left one another's orbit. I called him Priest because his lanky six-foot tall hippy-sphere looks priestly in the full length brown robe he dresses to match the oversized brown beret that droops off the gray hair side of his long as I can grow with my hair.

Priest, I think, is the very first person to ever hear me stumble through an early explanation of Baseline Economics. I boasted its significance, at least to me, but Bill expressed no interest. He annoys me that way.

"Priest you should play that thing," I encouraged him. That thing was a wind instrument, a plastic three octave keyboard he just carried around to look at. "Priest there are ten tourists passing by every sixty seconds."

Priest sits there rolling a cigarette composed from the butt-end tobacco of discarded factory-rolled cigarettes. He rolls the residual smoke in the same hunched over posture he uses when he digs through trash cans on Haight Street in full view of everyone.

"What the fuck are you doing eating out of trashcans, Priest? There is plenty of food!"

I yelled at Bill more than once.

I wrote this down for Bill on one of the sheets of paper I stole from the library copier. At the time I used the 20-pound bond to make paper airplanes I'd give to kids on Haight Street. Once a kid had a 100% paper airplane in hand, it was all Mom's problem. Oh yeah.

Oh, what did I write to Bill: "Argue for your weaknesses and sure enough they are yours."

"You've written that to me once before," Bill told me, handing the paper back.

I quickly folded it into a plane and gave it to a brunette just off work commute and holding a bottle of wine. "Here you go sweetheart, you're still a little girl, you know that..."

She took the plane, saw the inscription, and said: "I don't normally do this but you just made my day."

Two dollars later I looked at Bill and said: "This

street is swimming with money. With food. You just have to make people feel good, not just beg, beg, beg. Look all down about it. Boring. Hello? Who cares?"

"I knew you'd say something like that," Bill replied.

I didn't feel like playing his keyboard anymore so I handed it back to him. I felt bad like I always did when I got mad at Bill for being less than I expected.

"Bill, I know you think I'm always being dick to you but man, you are up there in age with me. We're freaking OG's. You have to leverage that. I mean, you're going to sleep on the street? Hard cement? Dig in garbage cans? Re-roll cigarettes from butts on the ground? I could get you a cigarette in ten seconds."

A nurse in scrubs walked by. She was off shift, not headed in, you could tell because her glasses had been removed after some time. I could see the red marks on her nose where the pair rested. She was heavily freckled.

"Hey there hot lips can I bum a smoke from you real quick?" I asked the nurse with my fingers pressed together. She abruptly stopped and gave me two American Spirits, waking away.

I handed them to Bill.

"There is plenty of everything," I told him. "Particularly food, man. Digging in trash? That looks fucking awful. It plays right in the hands of the worst homeless stereotypes, Bill. And you and I should be the smart guys."

I really didn't give a rat turd about who was smarter or not. I just wanted to give the Priest a leg up. Something like his age to leverage some sort of added confidence he could imagine, real or make-believe, that would give him more dignity and probably make his life better, if he'd try it.

But Bill just whines. He's never given me a hit a pot or a slice of anything but he always asks me for anything he wants. "Got any shards," Bill asks in code for speed. It sucks getting high with him because Bill has that drug fiend taint that restricts him from seeing that he's all take and no give. I hand him hits of my pipe all the time because I enjoy the older company.

"Can I get another taste of that?" Bill asks me when I put my pipe away.

"I'm done, man. I have to get rolling soon," I'll reply.

"But I'm not high," Bill whines, this from the guy who asks to borrow my cell phone to call his two daughters on Christmas Eve.

At night when I'm resting I'll think of this and get mad at Bill and imagine myself saying "well that's not my problem motherfucker." But instead all I generally say to Bill is "there's plenty of food, Bill."

I got the "there's plenty of food" line from Andrea, one of the Oak Street Three: Andrea, Scott Free and Paul the Garden Nome.

Everything is a total obsessive trip with Andrea. Like you've never seen. She knows all the details about everything and explains a situation to you like an auctioneer before you know what the subject is. She's vocal. Andrea's not talking to herself she's talking to the world, and there is a noticeable difference between the to. Andrea actually looks like she's holding a rational, passionate conversation with someone when she's just going over things in her head. She'll snap right out of it and talk to you like any litigator explaining what they've just done to fuck you. Or a talk radio host with no listeners.

"It's all wrong and we're "killing the bees" and the park will smell like piss again soon now that the rain has stopped and "you know that's what's wrong they're just thumbing their noses at the whole issue and nobody cares anyway because they have their fucking techy jobs" and "you know I have to feed this body and worry about germs and diseases."

You would never in a million years know that

Andrea is homeless, and has been for ten years. When she wants to watch TV she walks two blocks and sits in Dignity Health's emergency room and changes the channel to what she wants to enjoy. Andrea wears red dresses that perfectly match her bottom length dark brown hair which she ties behind her at bra strap level so her sexy rectangle glasses have the best opportunity to accentuate her bubbly Casper cheeks and red lullaby lips.

Andrea is the gizbar of the debt and booty of San Francisco's homeless confrontation with the housed. A wax Barbie in a burning dollhouse. She can't exist outside, she can't stay in much longer. Andrea is not accommodating to ending arguments. The girl cannot accept loss. She gets upset then teary that her mom and sister eat at The Olive Garden. To that, Andrea's not really what I would soon be referring to as a Baseliner. She has a heel firmly cemented in mainstream society that keeps the other heel from sinking into the mud. Not like the clan in denial and homeless limb. No. Andrea is a "normal" person preserved in perfectly housed form who slipped into homelessness and found it to be just another room to carve up the issues of the world in. She's the Queen on the chess board. Move any direction she wants. A very lethal, discombobulated tapestry of angry sixties activism and grumpy old man spit-talk.

Andrea has perfect skin, smooth as cream. She could pass for Julia Louis Dryfuss circa *Seinfeld* if she took off her Woody Allen frames. Her diet is terrible. She won't eat fruits or vegetables or pizza, and she's a shameless garbage digger, that's the only thing that outs her, and of course it has to be the worst offense. Andrea is light years ahead of Bill in her relentless garbage grabbiness. No waste can is too small or located in too populated an area for Andrea not to open up and pick through. In fact it takes you a moment to focus in on what you're looking at when you see Andrea digging through garbage. Did the poor dear accidentally throw her keys away when she tossed something in the garbage?

Andrea's also a collector, not a builder. She likes having stuff and it makes no sense to her why anyone would want to steal from her shopping basket. Cups and utensils, dresses, bedding, makeup, girl supplies, this thing she found. Drugs, money, food, electronics, forget it. Bothering Andrea's property just creates an annoying clutter.

Andrea lives off Oak Street, parks her shopping basket next to the M.A.S.H. unit Scott Free built. She drapes her cart with a large piece of cardboard upon which she's written:

Please do not touch Andrea's stuff.
This is her stuff and not yours.

I found a bike frame on its side next to a cardboard sign written in script I recognized which read:

This is the property of Andrea
who will be right back to get it. Please leave it alone.

I borrowed a piece of foam rubber from Andrea one night to use as a pillow. It was attached to her cart, not in it. I took it anyway, sleeping just across the street from where she would bed down later. I'd just broken up with Harriett. Andrea and I were getting along and I didn't think she would mind. I was right there, sleeping within earshot of where she'd make camp.

I was in a disturbed mood post-Harriett. I started mumbling or grunting in my sleep and the person on the other side of the open widow I made these noises beneath got tired of listening and called the police.

The cop woke me and ordered me away. Made Andrea gather her bedding too. Woken, she wasn't happy.

"And you stole a piece of my cushion!" Andrea yelled. "You know you don't want to fuck up out here! You get branded a thief and you get fucked! You don't want me having some guys smash your teeth into the back of your head with a two-by-four while you sleep, do you?"

It is possible to shoulder so much weight that the act of emptying a 24-ounce container of Glacier Springs water you've been carrying on the side of your backpack delivers the sensation of lift as the weighty water chooses gravity over you, and pours to the ground like sand from the bags of your rising hot air balloon.

"Squirrels don't have to cart around their nuts, cart around everything they own just so they can take a stroll through the park!" Andrea observed. "Why then should we have to?"

The load that your back can bear greatly determines your Quality of Life (QoL) as a homeless person. That foam mattress core you just slept so well on last night after it magically appeared on the sidewalk is not just a miracle but also a technical and physical challenge to lug around. The more stuff your carry, the sooner you have to bed down, the more you'll get woken in the middle of the night by cops who want to move you, and the more stuff you'll lose to theft.

Besides, having lots of shit sucks. Every homeless person I ever met who had something stolen told me that in the long run they were happy they no longer had to carry it. A laptop, a folding chair, a keyboard, sewing machine, backyard umbrella, a generator. Once gone they did not matter. Except for guitars. Have yet to meet anyone happy about losing a guitar.

The less stuff you have the more free time you're going to have to work with nothing. Working with nothing is the hydrogen atom of activities on the atomic chart of choices. It is composed of satisfaction.

Working with nothing is the domain of Jim, the Chairman of The Board. Jim sort of floats around like a Greek line cook on acid always dressed in clean, seemingly new clothes. Warm jackets when fog covers. Shorts and Keds when it's time to do the crazy dance in the drum circle. Screaming through the woods or trying to edge himself in next to 14 year old's so he can get a hit of their joint, Jim wanders around in apparently perfect shape, void of possession. Few people talk to Jim. Kids sneak up to him and scream in his ear to see if he'll freak out, which he never does. He's not welcome in popular pot circles because from what I heard he used to get stoned and masturbate in plain view of you. Harriett always talked down to him, giving him only the time for "hello there, James."

I began to collect stuff during my first few months, but gave up. Convenience did not outweigh inconvenience. If I needed tweezers or tape, anything, I'd ask for it when I had the time to use it. No planning ahead. Or it would just appear. Ahead of me on the trail above the roller rink. Seemingly only seconds there. If something was dirty it was dirty. But never a dust spec on anything. It all appeared moments before I arrived. This was happening to every homeless person I knew.

Anything I need I always get. It just comes to me when I need it and I don't think about it.

It was Natural Providership. The words came to mind the moment I made the connection. There was an active force at work on the homeless that kept them from ever being without a satisfied needs set. Delivering the missing bolt, the rare charger, the pair of jeans, the bacon cheese burger, the zip tie, all in the nick of time. It was spiritual. Here was homeless religion, or part of it. Why because this providing force didn't work alongside an indoor mentality. Doesn't work today.

Natural Providership.

This was the first physical force of Baseline Economics that I recognized and named.

The Law of Natural Providership

What is Natural Providership?

Natural Providership is the surplus of cause and effect.

Natural Providership is the industry of Mother Nature.

Natural Providership is only realized at Baseline, Status nullifies it.

Natural Providership never provides more than a moment requires.

When you release your thinking from the influences of time, calendaring, urgent desire and selfishness, and simply follow your intuition, the enhanced sense of cause and effect you attain ushers you to practically anything you need at Baseline, and nature works to bring it closer. To your joy, you'll discover that Natural Providership's path towards what you need is shorter and more enjoyably than any organized, downright determined effort to march forth and find it using your own fool-proof plan.

The faster you disconnect your ego from your absolute essential needs, the sooner you witness how well garnished the road of naturally winding cause and effect becomes with food, money, clothes, drugs, equipment, and encounters that avail your hands off the wheel.

This is Natural Providership.

Natural Providership cannot save you from foreclosure or front you a few bucks so you can party until you get paid. It is a force that fills vacuums of shared human surplus. Natural Providership balances and resolves consumption, production and discovery, which together create abundance. The miraculous power does not respond to artificiality. It will not offer up the unneeded, and cannot be fooled. If everyone's hair fell completely out tomorrow, Natural Providership would never again provide anything related to hair care. Not even a comb on the ground. Unless you want to make a mouth organ.

Natural Providership is everywhere, but it does not deliver to Status. In Status, there is literally no time for Natural Providership to work. Not that it wouldn't work in Status, as it's equal to all people. But Status is too overwhelmed by bad choices for a good choice like Natural Providership to break out, it being so low on the radar of Status. Status is too busy venturously making decision after decision, almost without stop, to sacrifice the convenience that bad choices typically offer.

All you need to do to ignite Natural Providership is make a sincere effort to absolutely focus on only what is necessary, then follow your natural intuition free of any outside influence. My average time to discovery of a need, about 15 minutes. I've never timed an episode with a watch, but I'm calculating from a four figure test sample.

Status is bursting with much louder bad choices, which are specialized for a specific tasks and can be in your paws before I finish this sentence. Stores are fat with bad choices gnawing for your discretionary and emergency spending. And you can factor time into these choices. Time until activation, cooks in 45 minutes, finished in three hours, six weeks for delivery. Cannot do this with Natural Providership.

I came upon a badly needed belt for my oversized jeans on a park bench. It even matched my pants. Took about three hours.

Discover you left your belt at home when you open your suitcase the morning of the wedding? In Status, there is literally NO TIME for Natural Providership to work.

Even in non-emergencies, there is no time. Status is not allowed enough time to think, because so much choice is being pushed at you from outside, and these choices want to be first. Natural Providership listens to you, to the guidance of choices coming from the inside.

Sorry, Status.

"Did you find the torque wrench?!"

"It'll be here. No worries..."

"Man, the fucking race is about to start! We're in the fucking pit!"

"I'm leveraging Natural Providership."

"What? I asked you to get one thirty minutes ago!"

"It's okay, it's okay. Shhh. I have to relax and you're working me all up with this. I'm gonna take another walk."

"Wha?!... Uh... Don't come back, dick weed!"

Nope.

Natural Providership can only give you what you need, mostly when you don't know it yet. Which is why you should think about everything you see. Not just glaze over it. For new Baseliners, it takes a few tries to sync up what you really need with what you're thinking. They'll be noise, but you'll get in. Once you tap Natural Providership examples of it at work become too frequent to recall. And since any manipulation of your pure instinct deactivates Natural Providership, simple recollections of it serve as guides for it's conjure. Needs that are naturally provided for must be genuine: Food (only when your body must eat – no unnecessary snacks), waterproofing, warmth, and tactical provisions like socks, zip ties when a pair of Levis provided to you on the street are plus three in size, an adapter for your iPhone or a set of ear buds (entertainment is a genuine need at Baseline), and marijuana or any other drug you are about to run out of because drugs accompany entertainment as a category of genuine need in Baseline.

A fascinating and eerie observation of nature's

care for Baseliners as part of the protected natural order can be found in the amount in which Natural Providership delivers free drugs to you when you are about to go dry. Perfectly balanced moderation is what Natural Providership breaks out. Left to the provisioning of Natural Providership alone, you would never have enough drugs at any one time to get grossly intoxicated, sick from excess, or dead from an overdose.

The spiritually relieving mystery of Natural Providership makes it difficult to image that this healthy metering mechanism for drug consumption in a no rules community is anywhere near accidental. There is simply too much functioning design to it, and too much love for the Former Child.

At its most basic rhythm, Natural Providership is exactly what you might experience during a perfect day, without ever being told Natural Providership was taking place.

You are given some free pot from Ziggy because he had "a good night" before it rained but the prescription eye glass case you keep pot in is full with no room to keep the new pot safe and dry. You have urgent thoughts about finding someone to trade the excess pot to for any food they want to trade because you have not eaten all day. But your pure, non-panicked instinct tells you to just go to Hippy Hill where you have no plan but once there, poof! There's a person you recognize with a friendly face who has an extra key-chain weed canister he'll break out from a SKU of them he found. He gives it to you so you can stow your extra pot and smoke a bowl with him (Note: This person has no weed and also found the canisters for free so Natural Providership with your unplanned arrival has kicked in for him too). Then as you head off to look for food nothing appears, but in a few moments look who's here, she'll feed you using the last of her food stamps. She does without asking for anything, and thanks to Natural

Providership your intuitive decision making delivered to you everything you needed that morning. It channeled from others. It channeled from you. And for skeptics claiming this is just trade and swap, Natural Providership operates alone, delivering with or without interaction with other people. Solitude summons a truly magical form of Natural Providership that you must experience, but remember that community multiplies the power of Natural Providership by the number of people you interact with.

If common mistake invalidated great work,
you would not exist.

Candy Rack

It's a candy rack. Same kind you see in a grocery checkout line somewhere near the register. Loaded with candy. I've seen at least one a candy rack of some kind practically every day of my life, since my mother began taking me as an infant to places outside our home. Candy racks are as recognizable as Trees, and together they tell us something.

To Status, so what, right? It's a candy rack and you're not thinking about me you're thinking about that Snickers bar to my left.

However, to a Baseliner, only a few months after departing Status, this candy rack is a blinding glare of information rapidly triggering the brain to identify colors, words, urgent artwork, health warnings, pricing formulas, dieting schedules, household budget calculations, flavor memories, advertising influences and reflexes like hunger, self-restraint, theft, guilt, nostalgia and self-pity.

That's a big drain on the brain, an organ which is going to sharpen its pencil and process all of the candy rack information it is allowed to sense, even if you personally aren't interested in the candy rack one iota.

This makes the typical candy rack a high voltage jump-starter for anxiety and the draining, repetitive planning that Status-borne self-doubt introduces. Your nerves get a tad more wound up just standing next to a candy rack, and that tension impacts your body like a pothole's impact on your car tire. Its unnecessary wear and tear inflicted over the long term.

Now, walk from our candy rack to a nearby line of trees in the park or forest and you'll feel yourself relax when you concentrate on this nature.

A tree hugger argument?

Nonsense. No one is saying the tree, or any tree, is any better than any candy rack. Admit what you see: The candy rack is clearly more exciting and enticing. More fun to play with. The candy rack rules. It's a combination of as many attempts to please you with candy as the rack can hold.

The tree doesn't do squat. It does nothing for you similar to what the candy rack offers, and the candy rack is just a guess. Someone's idea, imagination, of what might satisfy most of us at any given time.

The tree is on purpose. It has no concern for what satisfies us.

The differences in our behavior when near the candy rack or near the tree illustrates that bad choices can be, and are, introduced in our world by us.

What's missing from the candy rack is a visible choice for not wanting or needing anything from it. Not a small-print warning about a choking hazard in a particular candy, but rather a choice you can decide upon that promotes not wanting anything on the candy rack. There is no message anywhere on the candy rack that tells you its okay not to want anything from it.

You cannot walk away from the candy rack empty handed without apologizing to yourself or someone else.

The candy rack is composed of many delicious ideas from people aiming to sell you their product, so not selecting a candy to purchase somehow implies that the candy rack failed, the cumulative attempt by many to satisfy you failed, so you're draw to at least pick something if you have to, anything.

Thus, a bad choice appears. Fail to make a choice, even a bad one, and you introduce loss. You lost your chance to grab a sweet.

Bad choices play "gotcha!" with our decisions,

which should lead us to ask "What are bad decisions doing there then?"

And that's if you already haven't given up on this line of thinking because from a proper perspective of your abilities and resources you have unlimited choices and unlimited decision making capabilities.

The first – Your unlimited choices - is an absolute lie based on a play on words.

The second – Unlimited decision making capabilities - is 100% true all of the time all of your life.

You have never made a bad decision in your life. Even if it was not being able to walk away from a candy rack. It's impossible for you to have ever made a bad decision. You knew what was behind you, you knew what was in front of you. You knew your exposure to risk, who you cared for and who you didn't care so much for. And you were right there! How could you fuck that up? You couldn't.

You have never made a bad decision. What happened, if you harbor any regret, is you were not given good enough choices. You cannot give a person three bad choices and expect a good choice. The right decision will be made, but the results will only be as good as the choices allowed. You may be up to your ears in choices, but the possibility they all are bad cannot be ruled out.

Why would a sane society create bad choices for itself? Or allow sub-par choices to be installed and marketed as status quo?

And what makes a bad choice anyway?

Think of the Harlem Globetrotters. Curly Neal and Meadowlark Lemon, driving their fellow exhibition team the Washington Generals and the keystone referees crazy by twirling the ball on fingertip and squeezing the net so the rock can't swish through. Doing this, they didn't really break any rules in the rule book of basketball. Real referees would have created a log jam of fouls but wouldn't have benched players. Practically nothing the Harlem Globetrotters did was against the rules of basketball.

What we witnessed was the introduction and use of techniques that were not in the rules of basketball, that were not given as options to try, the rules being nothing but a list of the things a basketball player shouldn't do.

This is the perfect example of how bad choices are created.

There were no rules to tell you not to twirl the ball in an opposing player's face. So a part of the game evolved because there was no rule. There was nothing. So the game advanced as a cool move that wasn't written down organically took hold. It was clumsy basketball, acts like this were relegated to entertainment, but the sport nevertheless evolved and a good choice we were never told about was born.

The development of basketball came from the slow acceptance of better choices that were not outlined in the rule book as being choices you could make. The three-point line, we're looking at you.

Between the effort to decide upon something and the conclusive decision on what that something is lies the argument.

The argument is a product that we created by allowing self-doubt and imagination - instead of confidence - to police the enactment of change. The argument is a way to avoid loss, which we falsely believe we have control over and cannot accept. We have, as a society, never accepted loss since that moment the first person to ever make a conscious human decision refused to accept loss.

Why a refusal? That person long ago, like us today, did not know where a loss went. No matter what it was, or is: A person, love, thought, deed, action, purpose.

Troubling enough, even more so when you realize you and everyone else have no idea what this world you are in is, or expects from you.

That moment was the Big Bang of Status in human society.

The greater a person resists loss, the more that person has. Of anything. If a person does not have something they can still effect it and control it using a man-made mind game called The Argument, which is an irreconcilable loop of benevolent doubt that when relentlessly delivered empowers the imagination of the recipient with real-time control over their behavior, weakening the influence of any preplanned response or non-argumentative reasoning. And The Argument is fun. It could have been a very early language combat technique for verbal fights at distances close enough to be heard but not physically harmed.

The Argument controls a thing by preventing its conclusion, which is an end, a loss. So we argue our way back from loss. Always have. Just got better at it. Forgot what we were doing.

Each piece of candy on the candy rack can be exposed to an argument which throws any conclusiveness about it being the right decision directly back to your mind's debate room: Colors, words, urgent artwork, health warnings, pricing formulas, dieting schedules, household budget calculations, flavor memories, advertising influences and reflexes like hunger, self-restraint, theft, guilt, nostalgia and self-pity.

Mathematically and without factoring in the behavior of most people, with no choice listed on the candy rack to not buy any candy at all a person could be stuck forever standing there making a choice then reconsidering that choice for any argumentative reason, all of which would be deserving of an audience or a person that has been denied their right of validity. See the deadly cycle? Proceed to decide again only to arrive at a new argument, and back into debate we go.

This is our inability to accept loss. The candy rack is a compact model of zero conclusiveness. Of course no dummy would stand there forever making that kind of inconsequential choice, but we're modeling on a system scale here for sake of familiarity.

To no one's fault past or present we have let run wild a culture that cannot accept loss. This is the basic code error in our culture's algorithm. Nothing we create, say, or envision proceeds without being infected by this primordial fixation that arrives from a perpetually untended inconclusiveness of life after death.

Lose the Big Guy

He's the gentle giant you are going to meet at Baseline. He's saddened as an outcast from Status and wants back in. But no begging. He'll just stand there at the entrance to Safeway staring off into the distance through black wrap-around sunglasses. His bold bald head and navy blue plastic jacket will each look too tight on his shoulders. Without intention, he'll intimidate shoppers. and For this shoppers will reluctantly hand him something they didn't really need to buy in the first place.

He goes by Alex and after I bought him a can of Pabst Blue Ribbon beer he assumed I'd buy him one every time I shopped. He didn't react when I first said no. Its just that Alex makes it hard to work up to a no. He really scares you with his silence and unmoving intention. I'm a real giver so he must have had a hell of a time getting hand outs of anything. Fear's probably the only thing that motivated donors.

I liked his silent company and he liked someone listening and I fantasized a few times he was my tough guy, my strong man, the muscle behind me, my body guard, my debt collector, the person you don't want to see. Nah. Living outdoors does that too you. That imagination zone has been let wide open.

Instead of a flunkie, Alex was sincerely determined to give it the college try, enroll in San Francisco Community College. He carried a schedule of free classes teaching paying skills that could make rent.

"I'm excited to learn about something new," he said. It was an odd sentence coming from a man of his look. Even sounded weird, empty, like his heart really wasn't in it. He spoke monotone and flat. "Meeting new people," he added. Just as out of place.

For days he thumbs through the class schedule, always in the wrap-around s. He sits next to me on the hill overlooking the roller rink as I draft this book. Each day Alex has a different part of some machinery packed into his baby stroller. A water pump, a blow torch handle, the instrument panel from a Nissan Centra someone tried to roll back the odometer on.

"What's up with that gizmo?" I'd ask.

"It's a variac."

What I saw was a Frisbee-sized coil of copper wire with a large dial on it pointing to white numbers all the way around. Heavy gauge wires, red, white, black, sticking out from its rear. Looked like it weighed a ton.

"What is it a generator?"

"A variable transformer."

Alex had been a car salesman in Status. Made sense of the pattern of stuff he turned up with. He missed the job. He missed the people. He missed the life. He missed not having to think about it. I'd just asked him if he really wanted to go back to work.

"I want to get back to those days," he said, showing the first hint of enthusiasm I'd ever seen. "We had TV, and I could drive around in the car. I had a Honda and it was paid for. Great. We'd drive around and had a house."

Alex remembered his past like a paradise, which it certainly wasn't, at least by his standards. But memories of asking the boss if he could find any more room for discounting had taken on a holy radiance to Alex. I could feel it when he dreamed about it. They weren't memories, alone. Alex had enshrined his past in Status. Recalled it like a dead dog. Not recollections, a Universe for a dead existence. No way to enter it without a visible expression of regret.

No one will hire Alex unless they are forced. His eyes are to near burst capacity for any HR screener to risk opening his Pandora's Box.

"I'm changing careers to music," he told me, starting to lift the variac from the stroller but surrendering to its weight. "Engineering. I'm going to be a record engineer, who makes the sound."

"Cool."

"They have a class for it."

"What's that do?"

"I'm going to hook it up to an amplifier, like Eddie Van Halen did." Alex tore an old issue of *Guitar Player* magazine from his stroller. On the cover, Eddie Van Halen circa 1981 smiled with a cigarette between his teeth. "Says right here if you do that, like Eddie Van Halen here did, you'll make the tubes melt."

"Is that safe?"

He handed me the magazine. Three rolling papers fluttered from its flapping pages. Practically every paragraph of the cover story ended with Eddie Van Halen recommending that no reader dare attempt anything out of the ordinary with a variac, otherwise you get electrocuted dead. Your new career in music, over.

"This is why these things arrive," Alex said in reflection.

When Alex appeared with a fairly complex blood sugar meter heart/blood pressure monitor he was changing his career to health care. His mom had worked as an assistant to a veterinarian who worked for the Humane Society. Her role was putting animals to sleep, forever. The conveyor-belt job was delegated to her. She wasn't licensed to administer death, but heads looked the other way given the volume of animals in line to be taken down. Alex reported this as a testament to his mother's natural skill as a medical professional, able to do things other people had to be trained for.

I get lost in work for a while. I realize it's been what feels like three months with no Alex. Then he's back, and he's different. He's drifted off, let his mind go. The baby stroller of belongings he kept so neatly organized with class schedules is missing. No new gizmo with career path. A colony-sized swath of bed bugs cling in assembly to the pants leg of his red warm-ups, thick as a mud splash. I turn away. Gag. His once determined silence has become incoherent mumble, just loud enough for me to hear sitting next to him.

I don't have to test him with a question to know Alex is gone. I can hear the wind blow when I try to get inside his mind, hear what's up. Plenty of people I know have slid into la-la land since becoming homeless. I laugh at them, and with them. I have close friends who are totally, happily bonkers. But Alex makes me sad. Something over him is very unfair. Where others ask no pity for the nuttiness they exude, Alex is deflated. Someone validated his $80 million Power Ball numbers as winners then gave Alex 30 minutes of Cinderella celebration before telling him it was all a joke. The numbers were losers. So was he. Ha, ha.

Alex is no revolutionary. He's a car salesman who got fired while no other choices for earning power presented themselves. He's a little boy, a former child, who misses the regular approval and reward cycle of his job. And like a little boy, Alex's anger and resistance to being a homeless tired and wore down until cooperation became rest. Rest too unrewarding to do anything but pout in a room he can only believe he was sent to for punishment. He has no idea why he deserves this. He's loved. Is given food, beers, drugs, time to be listened to and talk out his feelings. But he's finished with the time machine. He doesn't want to try again. It wouldn't be fair to do that and have it all taken away again, at a later, weaker age. Alex is a victim of a world with no choices for people who want to call it a day, even when hanging it up would benefit everyone except a company trying to sell a second career.

If Alex gets lucky, finds a case worker and obeys them, saying yes to everything, he might make it back to Status. Might because a return to Status is a con job best performed by excellent liars and actors who can make a torn present appear unopened. Alex is not that guy.

Luck and a seriously motivated senior case worker. If he loses his mind before those two things have the time to act, society has failed an innocent former child in a hideously inhuman way. Alex is, well, big. A giant child. And like a child he asks anyone near for what he wants, and reasons not to care are piling up in him. Alex is barreling towards becoming exactly what he was taught not to be, a dangerous monster.

Monster. Indifferent, taking what it wants.

A very sad and disappointed little boy whose mom and dad taught to be kind, will have gone to sleep.

I never saw Alex again. I don't know why he showed back up.

The Basketball Coach

In 2010 Joel Branstrom, a high school science teacher and basketball coach, was told he would win some tickets to a college final basketball game if he made a blindfolded half-court free throw in front of the entire school assembly. Not knowing the whole spectacle was a school-sponsored prank that depended on Branstrom not making the shot, he actually did, and horrified children had to tell their teacher they had lied, and done so remarkably. There never was any prize tickets. Event promotion and invitations to the media had all been initiated on the confidence that Branstrom would not succeed.

He laughed it off in public, but this is what Joel Branstrom should have said to the student body right then and there:

"First, I just wanted to say thanks. Wait, don't stop listening because none of you are off the hook, oh no. But thank you for that thought, for having what surely were your best intentions. You at least kept me in mind, so I know where your hearts are.

"That said, what you did was wrong. You were given a bad choice. A few of you have said you'll make good on the tickets, but I believe those few of you rushing to do that, to find tickets I never really wanted anyway, I believe you're doing it because you're afraid of hearing what I am about to say.

"You have all just demonstrated exactly how we screwed up in shaping this society of ours, the big mistake we let ourselves make - and then let ourselves keep making, and that now affects all our other decisions automatically. That shapes our world. A world that leaves each of us disturbingly empty, like the emptiness I felt when I made that basket, only to hear everyone's cheers dissolve to worry, panic that what was promised wasn't there.

"The prize that led me to prepare for this day, even if it meant me doing nothing different at all, wasn't real. The prize that motivated this event, the fliers and posters, the guys from local news here with us, and all of you who planned to be here like you are, this elaborate, exiting experience to tell one's grandchildren about if it all came true, if the teach really did make the basket! Wasn't there... Was never there.

"Nothing but a facade. Nothing from the beginning. Happiness and ribbons supporting and masking a lie, a sick joke right to the very core. No question that it would all end happily too, right? Why?

"You counted me out. That's why! You counted me out, didn't ya? The prize was dreamy, the set was perfect, the experience unforgettable, the man incapable! And that's what will make this work. The man not good enough to do it! Even if the prize were real he couldn't do it!

"But life goes on, we have to do something once and a while for entertainment, so let's engineer this great thing so the failure can't lose. Why should you care if I'm man enough to handle knowing I probably won't hit a blindfolded half-court free throw? I'll never make one again. Not with any TV cameras rolling, that's for sure.

"How dare you assume I'm not capable of being satisfied with that truth? With any truth?! This is our society, where the lotto card tells us right on it that we are going to lose! Don't believe it? Then you'll be told you don't know how to read!

"Ah, to hell with all this! At least... Give me that...

(a struggle for the microphone)

"Dammit... hands off. You too, Shepard! That's right! Jesus Christ."

The American Homeless Companion

Accept Loss Forever

America is a society that cannot accept loss.

Cemeteries, memorials, the preservation of written history and its enshrinement. Remembrances, all manner of records of loved ones. We cannot even accept the loss of replaceable items. So insurance, self-storage containers, data backup products and so on now allow replacement to be available before an original is ever lost.

There are few things in America that celebrate loss for what it is: A stopping point. An end.

This is why we are haunted by inconclusiveness. Dissatisfaction. Where is a "mission accomplished" that really sticks? That really means it? Look at what this torturous denial does to you and to the expectations of all you love?

All of the things we desire to keep, cherished reminders, valuable assets, property, you name it, each began heading towards our possession as a reward. A list is needless.

Each product you protect was not meant as an ending, but as a beginning. You've completed a recognized leg of a larger journey, but there is no mention of finality. No way. We're gonna keep trucking, like it or not. Even if it means "your second career in real estate" starting at age 68. Where are our choices for accepting loss in a good way? Where are our choices to stop? Call it a day. Be happy with that career you worked hard at, and enjoy life? If we are simply dying for anything to do why can't we agree that replacement paths are not always products, but rather what we are thinking up? What we feel like doing. Even if it's nothing.

We already have these paths as a society so we are not taking ourselves seriously enough, or we are not strong enough to create a path that is as entertaining as another person's game. A satisfying game would reward us with a peaceful sense of immunity, permanence and rest. A more difficult and unhealthy game would protest loss and cheer on totally unrealistic "never say die" attitudes. To satisfy our insecure urge to "keep the ball rolling" all of our coaching from childhood, to the boardroom, and during old age calls for action on an unspoken and impossible assurance that nothing ends. We know it all has to end someday, but "there's always tomorrow" according to the poster in the lunchroom.

Even in retirement actors portray healthy gray haired seniors telling us in TV commercials that it's never too late to start a new career. That at any age continued education always improves your life. This logic is correct. But what if you are too old to try, try again? Or you simply don't want to? We have no choices to make decisions on these feelings that don't invite the shadow of uselessness, shame and inadequacy cast over a lifetime of being warned that quitting is for losers.

Wouldn't all this be simpler if we merely accepted loss? Calibrate our lives to continue on without what was lost, in a way that makes the best of a person's remaining time? Choices to end projects and obey lifespans which aren't haunted by some invisible 10-count that proves you didn't try if you didn't get back up? Acceptance of loss as something real, not something you can resuscitate.

Let's go back to the old man pitching the second career in the TV commercial. Career education for retirees. Is that commercial's advice really the best idea? Sure continuing education of any kind will improve grandpa's life. He could read an operator's manual for his new home heating system and it would improve his life. What's left out of the sales pitch are the details of the rest of grandpa's fruitful and happy life. Why does he have to go back to work? I thought he retired? What happened there? What system works an old man all his life then has no choices for him but to keep working if he's poor? Or get off his butt and do something if he has retirement savings?

And come on, let's open our eyes here. Grandpa's old. He may die before what family considers a hobby, awards grandpa a diploma.

Is it fair to simply ignore that grandpa's family will be left to pay the balance of that second career's educational program? Can grandpa even sell a house? Would you buy one from an old man? Does anyone care?

And not everybody ends a long career healthy and surrounded by family and savings and some measure of security. Most, yes most, get sent to pasture at some point when management decides they are no longer needed or profitable to keep around. Are these folks thrilled to have to jump into a new career and barrel towards a nearer end under new pressures like age discrimination and physical pain?

At Baseline, loss is accepted.

Loss is what it is, a subtraction element, not an addition. At Baseline, loss performs the job it's supposed to do when conveyed as an idea in language. Loss normalizes episodes in a person's life that fall away and disappear, right or wrong. Any separation is gradually cleared away. All memories stay eternally in perfect form for you to reenter any time. Nothing of your life is lost.

At Baseline your brain will enjoy a sudden surplus of time, which you'll waste at first arguing in your head with people you're pissed at, or who made you homeless. Once that noise gets digested by your noggin the short fuse anger it lit will be replaced by serious attention to something dear to you. Something that drives you. Even if it's nothing at all, nothing at all will replace dishes, TV, and other chores.

Like never before cause and effect will become traceable to you at Baseline.

Imagine only knowing the letter "B" and then being given "A" and "C" along with an understanding of the alphabet. Removing the compressing bookends (Hint: Clocks) from the present moment and eliminating time will grant you working peripheral visibility of "A" and "C" while focusing only on "B".

At Baseline, your heightened awareness multiplies the events you notice, so as you move to the next moment you're logically more aware of, and prepared to recognize the effects of the previous moment on the present.

Unclocked, this added level of observation of A and C visibility of past-to-present cause and effect, reveals enough information about the trajectory of your movement through events to prepare for where that movement should take you. This is not being able to see the future. What this demonstrates is an understanding that a person's actions from moments ago are a reliable blueprint for their actions a few moments from now. This applies to complex behavior at Baseline, not just guessing a direction change.

At Baseline, I noticed that dozens of common, time-coupled comments and expressions used in everyday chit-chat to humorize loss of control, were no longer necessary to couple mundane events together. Expressions such as "man this day really flew by" or "this thing is really taking forever."

The removal of time as an usher of conversation also meant I heard fewer commands that unleash anxiety, like "hang in there." It's amazing to see how much less stress is caused when a Baseliner says "see you later" versus someone in Status saying "see you at six." And it has nothing to do with how badly you can't wait to see that person at six.

Status has recently unleashed a few and more blasphemous abuses of time as a commodity to be bought and sold, and denied, and stolen. You'll never hear them uttered in Baseline. In Status they are verbal monuments to our illusion that time is manageable. They darkly introduce the idea that time can be taken away, by people. Given back like a gift, by people. The sentence:

Yeah, I got it all done yesterday. I came across a lot of found time and knocked it out by noon.

This says mankind sure has a lot of nerve.

Found time. What? How can this be a noun in a serious human sentence?

We don't think it, but we have deified ourselves masters of time. The impossible. We really aren't. Never will ebb, but we allowed to say it. As seriously as we want to be. Even in a life or death situation.

"Stop you said what? You found time?
Then find more and keeping piling time on so we can keep this mess in front of us!"

How dare we? Sure it's all innocent word play but it's in our thinking! In Status. Words decoupled from their numerical power, and the smoking gun of the algorithm that keeps us all slaves to perpetual industry left running way too long. Chugging along for how many generations when we could have already hit the stop button? Our inability to accept loss. The barrier to satisfaction.

At Baseline words are words. Revalue the words and you're lying.

"Boy, time sure is flying."

You're lying. Time doesn't fly, and you can't assign it.

A Baseliner would overhear that fly statement and utter "Huh?"

If you enjoy low level anxiety and waves of stress brought on by uncertain language that makes you worry you have to get there, or worry you're already late, then simply dismiss our verbal manipulation of time as nothing more than trendy expressions meant to lighten us all up.

My sarcasm meter just exploded.

It took just over a year to completely shed man-made time markers from my perception of life as it unfolded. I was long free from the metronome of clocks, which I realized did more to cause people to lose control of time than help keep it.

All my life I've heard people complain after checking the time that either the day is flying by, or it's taking forever. These and any number of similar expressions were mostly delivered in the context of accomplishment, exhaustion or anticipation without anyone recognizing they exposed something else: How we overburden ourselves with responsibilities and preoccupations by first fragmenting time with clocks, then acting like God and assuming the ability to know where time should stand if it doesn't satisfy us. "Hey time, we're all back here so slow down." This authoritative frustration has been massaged into mankind's DNA since the first tools began helping us forget we have no power over nature other than to wreck it.

Once the conditioning of time awareness and management went silent, my perception of the world changed in a very elegant, mortal and terrifying way.

Independence Day was here and my food supply that day would last another, so I rested. No store, no work, no library, no need to see anyone. I wasn't tired. I was energized in a very unfamiliar, ultra-passive way. I had reached The Crossroads of Commitment. My mind was staying in Baseline indefinitely. My body had no opinion. It was a feeling like the body you have when you sit down in the office chair of your new job, and when finally left alone for the first time you take that first, deep, conclusive breath of relief.

Time became a single moment for me then, unimagined. I did not leave camp. So from a fixed perspective with no interruption I finally witnessed life's unbridled procession in Earth's own motion. I didn't meditate or concentrate on time, just fiddled about my new camp free of any task that would have to be ended at nightfall. Mankind's clock was gone.

My perception of time's absence was a denser "now."

I named it, Dense Now.

The present, whatever it was doing, became visually thicker, more substantial. There was no change in color or motion, nothing new. And when I wrote the two words "nothing new" to imply object permanence, the word "new" triggered the description of Dense Now perception.

What's different is not what's been removed – time – but what's been added back. Something old. Very old.

The original words to describe this added thing that fills in the space left by time's absence are gone. I forgot them in this moment of discovery and did not write them down.

When I realized what I was seeing there was no stepping back to look at what was Dense Now, or compare it in real time perception before Dense Now appeared. But when I compared my visual memories of my new camp when I first arrived to the way I remembered it after Dense Now, the difference was downright creepy.

Life flow with Dense Now visualization stacks on top of itself vertically, not horizontally with ends of past and future. The mosaic of the environment around you becomes richer and deeper in a way, like many things in nature we simply feel are there but are hidden. I couldn't understand how to describe the way these additions hid. I had no language that equated to Dense Now's numerical complexity. "Our minds have only reached so far," was what I thought.

I had three writing projects in front of me when Dense Now discovered me. I've always tried to concentrate on one project at a time and not bounce my thinking around from project to project in mid-thought. But against my will or summoning, as Dense Now set in the three projects became a single thought, like watching three race cars travel side by side and knowing the details of each driver's dash board instruments. The point of recognition was when I tried to partition each project by instructing myself to "think about this one first, then move to this one..."

I was powerless to separate anything. All three projects were one single thought – my writing work. The order I'd deadlined them to was there in the single thought, along with the entire content of each job, what I needed to research, who I needed to call, all together like one job. It suddenly seemed silly that I'd estimated a whole month for all three. They'd only take two weeks to complete, all of them less a snag here or there which my Dense Now mind also factored in for me.

My mind fought this, even though the Dense Now view of my work flow couldn't have been more easily laid out. Here's the kicker. At first I thought this effect was coming to me, from out of body. Then I knew this effect was coming from inside me and I'd simply never called on it before. I shuddered in disbelief when I knew I was performing this level of thinking. Disbelief that I wasn't giving myself enough credit for my own thought capacity, like some manager returning to work and shocked to see new workers he never knew were there.

It was a joyous moment to be human. For an instant, total satisfaction. I'd been given a more concentrated focus on the now, which resembled the unleashing of more brain power, for lack of more eloquent description.

Baseline's absence of time as an order changed my physical senses of sight, sound, and my own reflection. When I looked down at my feet after a few days in Baseline I appeared much taller than ever before, at any height I ever remember being. I adapted to this visual change as quickly in my reflection as I realized it was permanent and unthreatening. If I was to look taller to myself than ever before, no worries.

That's early Baseline logic for you.

In the timeless focus of Dense Now, two realizations occurred to me at once. Realizations of the origins of our behavior.

The first realization that strikes after Dense Now adds back to you unlocked mental dexterity. You get paranoid. The fix is in. You have been had, and maybe so has everyone (you just can't confirm that last part immediately). The fix is in, someone messed with the hands of the clock, or made the mess by thinking it up. Someone screwed up time and it's been screwing with your decision making ever since.

Time measurement emboldens our illusion that we have power over time, but our application of time as a tool does the opposite. When first introduced, time measurement was a scientific and entertaining way to observe the Sun and how mathematics stay in sync with the Universe. But time measured by mankind, who manipulated the art for self-service, became shackled by the impatience of process, and in typical decay eventually gave people a way to delay doing things. With clocks you can tag chores with a time marker so when you update the boss on the chore's progress you can point to a future moment – thanks to the clock – when everyone, not just you, will be able to see the improvements or progress made over the hours marked, even if all activity on the project took place only in the last five minutes. Before clocks, this chore set aside would only be seen as idle and in need of starting now. Now, not later.

The second realization that follows the visibility of Dense Now is one of death.

At Dense Now death becomes real to you. You thought it already was, but not the way you do in Baseline. Before Dense Now death was in your future. Submerged in Dense Now death is with you, today, in the now, vertically stacked with all time and not thrown forward into the future. All manner of things we did not realize we repurposed as a time delaying buttress against the arrival of death, such as sleep, suddenly allow time to come splashing into Dense Now. Not past or future time – all time. One moment. Death can now really and truly sneak up on you, and this can be troubling after a life of trying to cheat it.

Memories made in Dense Now are also quite strange and deserving of more study. I can now compare my pre-Dense Now memories to my new ones. Memories recorded in Dense Now are recalled as framed in a diffuse circle, not squared to the edges like a movie screen. More like a fishbowl. The picture of the memory distorts to nothing past the edges of the circular mental projection of my past.

I also have to be more specific now about what I want to recall when I reach back into my memory. If, for example, I wonder what I did this morning, I now have to scroll around a little more to find something I did, or recall a process. I can't just think "what was I doing during *Meet the Press*" or at 8am? This means the more I pay attention to the present, the faster my recall is because my attention recorded more detail, not just time stamps. Another Baseline gift.

Ideally you will not know or care what day it is. We are so accustomed to scheduling that we don't try anything to compare it with. Work flow without time markers or deadlines. The result of faster completion without you even realizing it.

Natural Providership, the Crossroads of Commitment, Dense Now.

The more I learned, the less I understood.

I hate that saying.

Next Week on Nova: We Don't Know Jack

Nothing any person has ever created, at any time throughout history, has been a "look what we know!" invention.

Instead, everything, all of mankind's little mischief has been "look at what we can do!"

Test that statement: Medical and legal "practices" not "mastery." How fast, how distant, how strong, safe, lasting, big, small, real, unreal?

The true scientific answer to all these questions about anything when it comes right down to the chalk board is:

We don't know.

Do we know atomic energy? Have we mastered nuclear power?

No. We can demonstrate and harness it. List down from mankind's great achievements from there.

We don't know.

It's scary to think that should be as scary as it really is.

We don't know jack so we make it up using language. Often recklessly.

Unchecked, combinations of accepted language inaccuracies can snowball along the banks of an idea making the outcome far frostier than what was originally intended.

Yet we continue bending language in ways we dare not apply to numbers and the strictness of mathematics. Plainly in front of us each day are reasons this fashionable habit is frightfully dangerous. How a task that requires three hours to complete no matter can be done we're told "before you know it" or "in less time than it takes to say" or "in two shakes of a lamb's tail" or any number of ways language is used to distort time, or lie, or make us believe we know, "in a jiffy."

Have you ever wondered why you aren't truly satisfied? Why your satisfaction - yours and everyone's - isn't ordained above other measures of pleasure the same way "Love" is secured as the gold standard among our words for affection? Why everything that promises satisfaction falls just short of delivering it true, and lasting?

And while we're at it why are we all still raised being told to model our actions and make decisions based on fairy tales and nursery rhymes whose words don't stand up in court or defend you against the IRS? "Forgive and forget." "To your own self be true." "Good things come to those who wait."

These and many other seemingly playful abuses of language appear everywhere in our lives.

Read them closely and you'll notice most of them when taken literally are unfairly demeaning to the person saying them. "I got nothing."

Others do the opposite, suggesting people have God-like powers over time and mortality. "Nothing's gonna stop me now!"

Some discount the person all together.

A chemist creates a product for the first time, say fiberglass, and proudly thinks to himself: "Wow! I can't believe I just did that!"

Why not? Why have we allowed a knee-jerk reaction to not believe in one's self into our casual language?

God gets a bulk of the credit at truly Eureka! moments.

"Thanks go to God, who without I could not have done this."

Thanks often get handed over to undeserving

colleagues for personal and political reasons but the social symptom is the same: Professional self-deprecation by our brightest citizens, which a self-esteem coach would notice and say "What do you mean you can't believe it? You did it. You! No one else. You are the amazing ingredient! Nothing in your laboratory!"

"Did you write this?"

"Oh... Uh, do you like it?"

Why are we expendable to our own, or other people's creations?

We don't kneel and pray to all of our creations, but when we grant creations like houses and clothes the authority to represent by proxy what our value is as a person, then the applause and criticism we perceive from people, even from our loved ones, cannot be judged as 100 percent accurate, valid or helpful. A man standing in front of his mansion is not going to get the same response from you if he were standing in front of his tent. In our picture of this man there are too many attached interests that, like home value, we have given proxy authority to, and these interests pollute clear communication between you and the man, pollution composed mostly of things you want, or may want, from this man. If he were truly recognized as the divine creation, not the house, or some gizmo, no one would give a rat's ass what he was standing in front of.

We do. It's measurable.

We're the folks on the top of the food chain with the big brains who think stuff up and bang it together. But we have relegated ourselves to our creations for so long now that calling the rumble seat for every industrial product journey became the procedure politely ingrained in us. A strange patience that's born from some rickety "I'll do ya one better" recklessness that doesn't need the moment because it's already thinking up the next best thing.

We have subjugated ourselves to our creations for so long that descriptive language alone ("priceless" or "antique") can manipulate numerical value, making it possible that once a product is owned it can become more valuable, instead of being "used". If a product comes from far away add even more value. You didn't make it? Slap on even more value. A stranger's art is always more pleasing to us than our own.

What the hell is going on here?

Our disjointed definitions, our topsy-turvy self-esteem, our absence of forward guidance, our public display of people wrongly labeled failures for the purpose of keeping people anxious, fearful and enslaved to a job. What are we doing to ourselves and our society when we take expressions uttered by strangers so seriously that our perception of value can be adjusted along with even the value of ourselves?

Us, we, always the least valuable part of the equation.

The answer, within our thinking, is that flawed line of code.

Whoever - and he or she was a good person probably doing what the smartest people around all agreed to do – introduced that line of code in our collective heads, that early spec of mortal fear written into our social algorithm, was trying to get a lot of things done by people unsure of doing anything. Left intact that line of code stunts our output, so we prove to ourselves we're unworthy of perfection, which must mean our hearts are simply not into it. We are not worthy of satisfaction. We cannot accept the means to its end.

"But I can accept loss."

No, you deal with it.

We can find personal closure in our loss of beloved Uncle James. But in mourning him we lose nothing and stick to what's certain: death. Preserving Uncle James's memory, legacy and teachings (his life, so to speak) can only be accomplished by preserving the time in which he lived and preventing the loss of things and customs and beliefs that were the foundation of what he bequeathed to us, operated upon.

This cycle of preservation of time, in a vastly unsynchronized way across the planet, has driven cultural progress into a log jam of arguments, in a very real way halting social progress altogether.

Note Facebook, et al. It is not social progress. It is social media. It is social automation. Really. A computer reminds you of a birthday, of people you might know even if you aren't thinking of people you might know. If you did, but do not.

Fewer people in fewer generations are witnessing in their lives significant social change that they knew would vanquish a clear wrongdoing. People can now live their entire life without a collective affirmation of shared hope. Only personal hope. Selfishness.

For us, solving anything marks an end to our quest for it.

Arriving at this end means breaking down the set ups of perhaps an epic of the search for what was rightly ours. An epic search that bound us together. And if we accept its loss, the set change is unbearable to the heart, whose job is to dare us to find ourselves heartless for being able to live without what we lost.

As a culture, layers of people – us, we – enacting protections designed to reduce loss has led, over time, to a hard-baked society that cannot accept this bundle of loss as a culture, or any combination of loss. We cannot let it go.

This is the cornerstone truth within *The American Homeless Companion*. This is the root malfunction entered into our social algorithm. All social and personal shortcomings we experience run home to this truth and its causality. All that we've built around us, and all that continues to be, is stunted to the same refracted degree just below satisfying.

You know this to be true.

We are a society which cannot accept loss.

At Baseline you can at last grasp this with some equitable measure of confidence.

At Baseline you can perform you own type of root cause analysis free from anxiety and time and fear of losing your food and housing. You see clearly The Big Three Things People Have Got to Lose. The Holy Trinity of Status:

Privacy, Old Wisdom, and The Argument.

It's as simple as that.

Disagree?

Join us in homelessness.. We have lived both sides. Have you?

"We know what's bugging you, kid... It's that itching, ouchy, yucky, reeking, did you hear that? sticky, buggy, what was that? turn that thing off, unshowered feeling..."

Golden Gate Park, Saturday afternoon:

A four-year old girl walking with her mom sees a woman wearing glasses and a man relaxed on the park's sprawling grass lawn, having lunch and laughing as they recline on an expensive inflatable camping mattress. They're sharing a bottle of wine with cheese and crackers neatly spread before them.

The lawn is happily filled with identical picnics being enjoyed by all different kinds of people, families, orientations, dreams.

The woman wearing glasses hands her wine glass to the man and from a classic wicker picnic basket lifts to offer a lollipop in sealed clear plastic like the type given away at a pediatrician's office. She holds the fresh candy up as an offer to the little girl, who begins to walk towards it.

"Look mommy!"

Mom grabs the child's shoulder and refuses to let go.

The woman wearing glasses is homeless.

How does mom know this, and the child does not?

All of the dozens of picnics on the lawn are different in color, size and participants. Each has fundamentally the same gear. Something to spread out and lay on, food and alcoholic beverages, blankets because it's chilly in San Francisco, maybe some music. Everyone is getting along and visiting with one another as they please.

What tipped mom off?

If it was just the sleeping bags on the couple's

backpacks then why would Mom prevent her child from taking a lollipop from two European tourists hiking around Northern California? The city is full of them.

Like most mom's, our mom could have allowed her child to take the lollipop just to be nice, then having any doubts discarded it for a new one. Happens every Halloween with apples.

How did mom know the couple was homeless, when the child did not?

And the bonus question: What was om afraid of?

The answer is made for moms: Nothing except the way the couple smells and the food they are eating is fresh. That's it.

Fresh is not the word you were expecting, was it?

Fresh covers all ground except any added scent like perfume, which is an addition, not a subtraction like not using shampoo. The couple has great clothes, nothing worn by mistake, but the clothes are not freshly cleaned. Their hair is fashionable for the city and groomed correctly, but it is not freshly washed. Mom makes lots of yucky assumptions about hygiene beneath the couple's outer wear, then looks at their gear. Everything, the lunch basket, the mattress, wine glasses, are all expensive versions designed as luxury items. But none of them is freshly manufactured. If someone simply argues you can't have a couple on a bed with their belongings in the park if children are there too, I'd agree. They are right. No one should make assumptions that they can hang shit that most people have a closet to contain all over tree limbs in the park.

Baseliners are not here to demonstrate a lack of caring about what we all know people are commonly offended by. That's just being a shit-disturber. On the other hand, equally and fairly, parents should not take their kids to the park unless they are prepared to talk to their child about what they see, not move on to more fun stuff by dismissing your child's wonder. Talk about what's going on, even if you have no idea. Just be compassionate. It's your kid for God's sake. Who knows until you go up and talk to them?

What if the couple on the mattress were flamboyantly gay and openly kissing as an expression of love? You wouldn't dare refuse the candy, or dare suggest they leave like the homeless couple should, would you? "Look Mommy, it's a gay homeless couple... I think..."

Don't like it and don't want to talk to your kid about it? There are lots of places elsewhere in the park. The Baseline couple was there first.

No one has the right to make anyone uncomfortable.

Let's review: Baseliners know how to cook a meal in a kitchen, make a bed, pay a bill, lock a door, clean a room. Does Status know how to find a comfortable place to sleep at night in Golden Gate Park?

Many, many people you would call homeless do not want to go back inside whatever it is you think is a house. These people, these Baseliners, these homeless of yours, they don't want to talk about why they have no interest in reentering Status. Our language has fallen out of alignment so the discussion of a Baseline's economic goals has been a demoralizing pain in the ass. But that is about to change.

If you are not unhappy about being dirty, you don't care. If you don't care, you didn't listen.

As a society that cannot accept loss, most of us have been trained to believe that cleaning, and the use of multiple cleaners, is part of the operation cycle of all things, even plants and animals. Note: The operation cycle, not the maintenance cycle. They are two distinctively different cycles of existence and cannot be one, unless a third maintenance cycle is added, at extra cost. Any "self-healing" machine (be it a PC or an oven) shuts a part of itself down to replace, repair or update, but we are still sold on the idea that operation and maintenance can be performed simultaneously as if both cycles were taking place at the same time.

It's late July as I write this.

My body has been slowly, and at times painfully, making adjustments back to what must be its original factory settings. A showroom fresh shimmer.

An indestructible cleanliness has set in. It's amazing. I have reeked in the past drifting from state to state with broke punk rock bands in four day old socks, two weeks of sour smell trying to trust rock salt as a deodorant. Always really trying to cover odor that only appeared after applying some product. Now no part of me is smelly, and I've smelled a lot of smelly smells.

I've always had something on me smell incredibly awful at times all of my life in Status. Balls, feet, underarms, breath. I threw wads of cash at these retched odors. Stuffed extra socks into my pockets before dates. Looked like a fool chewing gum, crushing mints, or sneaking breath drops.

For a year and a half now I have gone without a shower and I smell just like someone with no smell on a normal day in San Francisco. No fragrance. No smell. No stink. Neutral odor.

Each morning at either the Conservatory of Flowers or the municipal tennis courts club house I use the restroom paper towels to wash my hands and arms and armpits, my face and my crotch, balls, front and back above the belt line and once every week I'll remember to brush my teeth with water when the ivory tongues plaquish. These facilities are generally vacant in the early morning but lines never stop me from stripping down and rinsing off. The tourists keep their distance, pass on washing their hands when I offer to step away from the sink. Locals will rinse their hands under sink water while I'm standing in front of it. The young white-collar locals hate me in the restroom. If I'm standing waiting for the sink or the stall they turn and walk out. Older locals wait like stone monoliths expecting me to obediently hurry up and get out of there way. I'm talking the whole time, making light of the whole thing. Kids staring get: "This is the way to go, little man! Quick rinse and off I go to play outside! Right, dad?"

An fellow with a group from Singapore uttered the "B" word after locking himself in the stall. He should have used the one on the tour bus.

"Hey, a man's got stay clean," said a guy in mid-life crisis wearing a tennis outfit and taking a leak.

"Yeah, it doesn't take Nelson Mandela to recognize a serious civil rights issue!" I hollered, echoing off the porcelain.

McEnroe raised his right fist.

I never noticed how quickly I got dirty until I stopped showering. First off I was homeless, so I reckoned "what the fuck." If I had dirt on my jeans, smelled a tad sour, I had a perfect excuse for it. This opened the door to one pair of clothes. One of every wearable. Wash clothes in the nude, or replace items as needed, throwing the old threads away. Disposable clothes.

A certain 99% of all Baseliners carry unneeded, duplicate clothing. Even if it's just socks, which can be found in minutes. Anyone will go into Fred's Market and buy you a 99 cent pair of cotton socks if you ask them. They will ring in up with their purchase if you are sincere, and to keep you honest you homeless drunk you. I'm not giving you any discretionary spending.

Girls like to change clothes and who doesn't like that? Clothes are free so what to do? As long as you aren't assigned the task of totting someone's full wardrobe around all day. Men should take advantage of the fact that men in San Francisco dress like superheros. The same clothes all the time, for almost any occasion. Accessorized uniforms. Necklaces, rings, boots, belts. The wealthiest people in the city dress like this. In the back of our mind we excuse them assuming they are so wealthy they buy seven sets of the exact same clothes so they aren't doing laundry every night. But they only have one pair, maybe two. College males, six-figure Bohemia techies, why can't the homeless see this and make that one pair of clothes they need look excellent. Put all your energy into that one pair of clothes, don't lay down on the street or in dirt while you're wearing them. Be super hero. I know Baseliners I wouldn't recognize if they changed clothes. The efficiency, the conservation of it all, the spotlight branding and higher, positive social profile. Looking like you belong. Baseline has many superheros. Just not enough.

Late in my second year I didn't think laundry mats should be part of being homeless. Friends collected extra clothes, scarves, long johns, and washed loads of them regularly at the Laundromat laundry mat on Waller Street, home of the Laundry Nazi. You can get practically naked at the Laundromat if you leave a joint on your dryer for Chris, the Laundry Nazi, and if you don't mind Chris' snotty, draconian rule.

I washed clothes there twice, that was it.

"That's a gang sign, dude," Wiz said as we sat on the steps to Laundromat one morning, me there to wash clothes after about a year hiatus. "That's mean stuff, man."

Wiz was talking about the spray painted "X" at out feet, in red and there long enough to fade. A "S" occupied the left and upper quadrants of the "X." An "S" occupied the right and lower. It was the tag for the Sf Dogs. Laundromat was their turf.

So what.

While Wix polished off a droopy bag of boxed red wine, I sat inside watching the washing count down, nothing over me but my leather jacket. Chris walked in. He was always leaving.

"You have a shirt?" the Laundry Nazi's Queenie voice asked me. There was a posted No Nudity policy on the wall next to No Alcohol and Last Wash is at 8:30pm.

"This is a shirt," I explained to the Laundry Nazi who is by no means of German decent or a supporter of genocide. He's a Seinfeld Nazi, ala Soup. He makes it hard for you to ease through a chore the way you would enjoy a simple pleasure in life.

"Why's this dryer running?" the Laundry Nazi asks everyone in the room. It's the only dryer running, and he hasn't been open long enough for a washer to complete a cycle. Do Not Dry Unwashed Clothing.

"That's my stuff," a kid wearing a Prince t-shirt confessed. "It's clean stuff. Just got wet last night."

"It's wet clean stuff," the Laundry Nazi thinks. "Alright."

As he shuffled towards the exit a man with a German Sheppard and an armload of sheets appeared at the entrance.

“Nice dog,” the Laundry Nazi said to his No Animals sign. “Next time keep it at home.”

The instant the Laundry Nazi was gone the kid in the Prince t-shirt hurried to his dryer and tossed in his sneakers which began to thud and click tumbling round and round.

No Shoes In The Dryers.

The second and last time I patronized Laundromat was a special day.

I was in the library that morning. I was itchy and thought it was withdrawal from alcohol which I'd stopped drinking because I'd yet to balance my Baseline budget. Using the restroom I lifted my black shirt up and saw four droplet-sized, itchy gray ovals of goo doing something there between my tits. Nondescript oily creatures with no visible leg or head. Gross.

I freaked, but the freak fell away. What were these pests doing? I turned on the sink and pinched the bugs off one by one, squishing them between my thumb and forefinger, flicking them into the sink desperate to examine them. They were all smashed up. Down the drain they went.

I splashed my chest with water. Turned on the hot air dryer to make normal noise for anyone waiting for the toilet. I examined the rest of my body for bugs. All I wanted to do was strip, shower, disinfect, swim in the ocean, neck deep in a scalding hot tub, wash my clothes. Burn them. Scream.

Someone knocked on the restroom door.

I collected myself and don't remember my rush to Laundromat, only three blocks away.

I only had a twenty dollar bill and not matter how panicked I was nothing was going to get me to pocket around $17.50 in quarters after I got out of there. The Laundry Nazi couldn't break it that early.

"There's an ATM that way," he instructed me. I knew which way "that" was.

Returned, stripped down to a bandanna that tied my sleeping bag to my backpack, staring at the washer on guard with a paper bag holding my wallet, a video camera and other pocket stuffers, I overheard someone bitching about dropping money on the floor.

"Where the fuck is it? What the fuck?"

Its an Sf Dog slapping both front pockets, scanning the tile around him. Yelling at is girlfriend who I'd made eye contact with.

"It was right here!" He mumbled a number I couldn't make out. "Hey, OG! You find any money on the floor?"

He's looking at me.

I shook my head no.

"What's up, OG? You got my money?" he said, walking towards where I sat on a wooden bar stool, naked. "HuH?"

"I don't have it, man. I didn't see any money."

"Okay show up then," he shakes his fists out, talking faster. "Show up!"

Three feet away he wants me to show him the

contents of my wallet, anything.

"I don't have it, man. I'm broke."

A second of the way he started to act had me reach into the bag for my wallet, which I flipped open to show $17.00. I slapped it closed back into the bag. He inched towards me.

"See you got it! You said your broke!"

Then he came at me so at the same time I cradled the bag tight. Off the stool I went, hitting the cold cream tile in front of a dryer I had open to use.

"I didn't take your money!" I screamed, pissed off. Fuck who he was. I wasn't going to fight.

He kicked me in the right ribs. Started to reach for the bag.

"He had twenty dollars when he came in here," the Landry Nazi, reduced to just "Chris" when a Dog was doing laundry, said.

Chris then walked out the door.

Dog boy wasn't taking the bag. He couldn't pry it out of my arms. He kicked me again.

"Do you know who I am?"

I didn't, but wasn't going to admit it.

"Yes."

He huffed, said "freak", and walked out. His girl was left folding her underwear.

I never saw bugs like those again, that big and in such few number. Tiny bugs come in sets of 10 to 20 critters. I you think you couldn't handle this, you are wrong.

Nothing about having bugs share your body is uninteresting. They tend to disappear about the same time they become interesting, about the time you wake up in the morning excited to see what's crawling on your chest or around your waistline. No product can rid human-born bugs without fertilizing a new growth cycle at a perpetual cost. So chill out. Dismiss them each morning. Trend their numbers.

Common bugs lay sand-grain eggs in your shirt and pant seams. The fabric on your back. Found one in my beard. Instead of making you feel like a filthy primate, parasites using you for survival should trigger the opposite effect. After all, you are the big giant animal thing, vastly more complex and certain to survive, if not forget, encounters with puny, barely significant creatures. Alas, they are one with you.

Get this through your noggin and bugs lose their repulsiveness.

There was nothing I could do to rid them, so I groomed them away each sunrise as a matter of routine. New arrivals. Sometimes three, sometimes thirty. Gone to that Great Follicle in the Sky with the pinch of two fingers and a far away flick.

I stopped deploring mosquito's, rare words from a Florida boy. Now, after the first few bites I only want the buzzing little vampires to stay out of my face. Surrendered to them, my back and arms have endured so many punctures that my skin feels like braid. I've stopped itching myself with the exception of one place. Where the rubber hits the road.

I almost killed a mosquito about to stab my pinkie toe, then I recalled how freaking orgasmic it feels to scratch a bite between toes. Ummm, that's it, right there, harder, run a nail over it, until your skin strips off. God it feels good.

So I let the little bugger inflict.

Never, ever, scratch your face.

At Baseline your body will begin to change before your mind does, and you'll notice this through your skin's tissue disablement and recovery. Your body will strengthen its follicles and calcium nails. It will re-balance calluses to pressure points, like that place you sit on your ass every night because you don't have a sofa.

Your natural chemistry will reclaim overall management of your skin, digestion, and complexion. The uncomfortable boil on your ass and the spider bite filled with puss on your arm will be recovered, and the armor will reappear a more appropriate derma.

Breath in these physical and mental changes presented by Baseline. You look worse the more you resist. Never feel sorry for yourself.

One filthy, resistant mess was this little speed freak long-haired fuckup I bought a slice of pizza for one afternoon thinking he was listening to me. I try to be a role model of independence.

Kids will be kids, but the young, sticky, obliviously greenhorn Baseliner who looked like a bad yearbook photo from 1971 was what the comedian Artie Johnson would describe as both interesting, and stupid.

If you catch a lost kid's eye and give them a confident nod, clumsy Baseline newbies will inch forward and stand next to you if they sense experience in the wild, or predict a free hit of pot. Silently they'll wait for you to continue whatever conversation you were running inside your head that was leading to giving them something. If they speak it'll be about Dead shows, how they got busted one time, or they'll just yell at their abused dog.

This kid arrived understanding little about the world beyond media's encouragement to build your very own cocaine empire, then shoot everyone who crosses you. He frightened himself when Baseline reminded him he was flesh and blood.

"Maybe I should just go to the hospital? I've got bugs on me. I'm dirty," he cried sitting on a curb in front of Happy Doughnuts.

"I wouldn't just go check myself in, or admit myself anywhere. It's just like jail. You're not going to be comfortable, or medicated as quickly as you need to be in that situation. If you are worried about your clothes, they'll disappear there and you'll be walking around in scrubs. Maybe you'll disappear? You think anyone is going to miss you?"

I got a rise out of scaring him, he deserved that little sympathy.

"No. No money," he mumbled with his head in his hands.

Then he made this stupid brag about how his worry soothes a so-called "heroin problem" and I want to laugh. Bullshit. Fuck you and your phony heroin habit. Go back to New York to your living parents you piece of shit starting to cry thinking I'm going to do what, give you something you dumb motherfucker?

He started to cry.

"I'm tired and there are bugs all over me."

"So?"

"What do I wear?"

I assume he's still tuned in to the idea that if he'd just wash his fucking clothes in the sink somewhere he would feel slightly better about himself.

"What do I wear?"

"Nothing. Boxers. Stand there naked and say hey I'm washing my clothes motherfucker."

"I don't have boxers."

"Jesus. Just wash one thing at a time. Pull down your shirt"

"How do I dry anything?"

I asked this same question to a pair of older Baseliners on the corner of Haight and Masonic where I'd fled away from this disgusting little punk. "A Tree?" is what these guys guessed, laughing at me.

The kid turned out to be a flake. Wanted $20 over the pizza to "try and get a little something going" which was code for buy $20 of some drug and deal it out to a profit. $20 of anything can be parsed out to earn $50, or at least double if you're a customer as well as a dealer. I fronted him but he shit on me. Told me three days later having a Molly revelation that he'd pay me "whenever Dan, because I'm seeing God right now, it's clear. So clear."

A day later he wanted me to kick his ass.

"Show me then, man! Break out whatever it is you use! Come on!" he encouraged me like a threat. Insinuating I had some secret weapon or Kung-Foo move I whipped out after everyone else is laying around with their shit kicked? I'm dangerously silent until then. Appearing weak until I produce from my jacket a spiked medieval hammer and chain? Too much violent entertainment. This is reality for this child. He grew up wanting bread and was force fed cake.

The last I heard about him was from Crazy Dave, who for reasons I didn't have reassured me one afternoon that he'd swung full force to the back of the kid's skinny neck a two-foot Craftsman adjustable pipe wrench.

There is no false confidence.
There is no false bravado.
And here's our favorite: False positives.
There is only confidence, bravado, and the positive.
Your senses are not false.
You are not to blame for the things around you.

The American Homeless Companion recommends chowing down on whole foods like apples and oranges from a dozen free food banks in San Francisco. All you can carry out. No register, no questions asked.

An assortment of fine menu items from some of the world's best restaurants are coming to you directly from diners bored of carrying warm to-go boxes.

Haight Street eateries are orchestrated by wait staff who automatically pack leftovers of any kind to send out the door with customers who'll tire of holding it and give it to a Baseliner. This practise is not as benevolent as it sounds. Whipping out to-go boxes keeps "the street people" from ruining the dining room view. Feed them and they go away.

You can't blame the eatery because it's rude to blatantly post outside a business entrance with a view holding depressing cardboard signs asking to be fed. Give diners some space. They are not there for you, don't think your funny, don't want to be entertained by you, and are starting to hate you. How much is your tip now, Mr. The World Revolves Around Me?

It's the kids usually doing this in-your-face posting. It's visible of mom's influence. Kids hooked on consistent and compassionate meal schedules. It illustrates just how short a time most have been away from home. Their Crayola Crayon signs could be notes on a suburban refrigerator door. "Can I have blueberry waffles with bacon?" "I'm hungry for anything today."

Eating is instrumental. If it's not meant to be eaten by hand, don't.

Streaks your clothes with food stains, looks pathetic you choking food down, and you eat too fast when you eat by hand. Always carry a fork or a spoon. If nada, tear a piece off the lid of the to-go box. Cup it like a Japanese rice spoon, shoveling the food in from the rim. Save napkins for hands and your ass. A wide knife performs all utensil tasks.

"Hey there, if you're not gonna eat that
I sure would love to help you."
- My pitch line

There are easier ways to get free food than begging. Food stamps. Nutritional assistance to the tune of $150-$300 and up per month provided via EBT debit card to anyone over 18 who confesses to be homeless. That's the only question the welfare office asks beyond your identification information, which you can say was stolen. The girl behind the glass window with the monocle won't cast any doubt. Won't even look up from her keyboard.

"Address?"

"I'm homeless."

I waited. Leaned forward, ready to listen. Please don't let anything go wrong.

Type, type, type. Nose scratch. Enter.

"So," she began, looking up. She raised her brow and sterling silver monocle fell from her right eye socket, stopped by its chain. "You live in..."

From her expression I gathered I was supposed to answer "San Francisco."

She nodded in encouragement.

"San Francisco," I said.

"Good. So you'll be buying your groceries in?"

"San Francisco."

She stared back at the computer, placed her eyewear back in.

"Let me see if the computer will give me a pro-rate for the short month," she explained, setting out with the mouse.

No. Just stop. Leave it. Don't give the computer a

chance to fuck up.

Next to the calendar there was a photo of the outside of the welfare office we sat in. I'd stared a hole in it but hadn't thought much about why it needed to be there.

"Follow my finger," she said from the screen. Then she pointed to the calendar, looking at me.

"Here is the door you came in from, recognize it?

"Yes."

"Walk back out and turn right. Go back in the third door you come to," she said as her fingers walked from door to door, middle finger lightly knocking on my destination door.

"There they will give you your card. Any questions?"

"When does it go in?"

"You are the ninth of each month, $179. Make sure you use the card and not let it go idle."

I sat there. Took a breath.

"Thank you," she said without looking up from the screen.

Tree hasn't seen his EBT card in six months. His reloads with $179 every third of the month. He gave the card and his pin number to a family near Daly City who pay Tree $150 cash in return. Tree prefers drugs over food. Food he harvests every night from residential trash containers he picks through for valuables and recyclables. After hanging around Scott Free's camp a few months, Tree left for Berkeley running from a death threat. He let his books with the San Francisco Dogs get too complicated and too much in the red. The Sf Dogs are a San Quentin prison gang who operate and finance speed crews in Golden Gate Park. They play prison rules. Stay ahead or get swatted to the ground while you're not looking. Get your ass kicked if you become your best customer and think you can rationalize it. Don't look at their girls, or their dogs.

Tweeker Tree let himself get way behind. $600. All he had to hear was the word Lumpy to haul tail out of San Francisco.

He doesn't have to come back to grocery shop.

The Bittersweet Sounds of Status

Spitting
Door locks
Purse snaps
Conversation halts
Dog growls
Shameful whispers
Children being told no
Dogs being told no
Huffing
Security guards
Cowardice
Mismatched Status symbols (poor driving leased Escalades,
rich in clean hipster wear)
Awkward attempts to look young
Diverted routes around you
Police stares
Pricey exercise products used a few times then sold
Averted eyes
Slack jaw gawking
Sheer disgust
Jealously (the old)
Admiration (the young)
Wild animals that don't run away
Plants sprouting from cement
Insecurity
Impatience
People worn out past their age
Tucked in smart phones (the ball and chain of society)
Complete ignorance

Okay, so surrounding my sleeping bag is a line of coyote brush forming a horseshoe wall and a 10-foot ceiling. Behind this foliage I've ample room to slide around on my rump, write, eat, and entertain a guest while deceptively camouflaged from view. To get a level seat on the hill I sit with my butt on the ground, then on a rolled up paper shopping bag from Safeway where by butt meets my thighs, then I place below my thighs a paperback copy of Steven King's *Needful Things* which Hector (who I loaned $15 to but wouldn't spot me a quarter) gave me to read and keep.

This shoring beneath my rear can be adjusted to form a perfectly level seat looking over the rink. The surface's fairly steep angle presents several advantages once you a) install a stop to keep your feet from sliding into the front bushes and b) fashion some basic levels to support drinks and prevent anything round from tumbling away. A steep angle also gives me surprise advantage over unwanted visitors who can be sent tumbling with one sudden lunge down the very uncomfortable hill scape.

It's impossible for anything, racoon s, people, cops, to get near me without making telling noise through tangled limbs and brush.

I sleep on natural cycles at Baseline. When I'm tired I zonk out. But I've always got one foxhole eye open in case a fellow Baseliner stumbles over my sleeping bag or steps on my face, explaining to me he's looking for "that buried box of dope that's here somewhere. I know you weren't asleep when I walked up. You're supposed to make a sound, so I know I'm not gonna be jumped."

This how I met Crazy Dave. An older, skinny ruffian too mature and with kids to be a lost-cause

Tweeker. But he'll never say no to drugs and alcohol, which amp up a creepy babbling psycho side of Dave. He's another who'll frighten the boots off you if you don't get it through your mind they are former children. It's not hard to be honest with people in an easy-going way that befriends you. Then you can get close to them without fear of being hit. You never see it coming.

When alone Dave comes down to Earth and avoids questions about his two teenage kids and talks in a very soft, gruff, polite voice. All lot of people are afraid of him. But his age - 45 - marshals needed leadership amongst the young and the worthless.

Baseliners don't report being groggy when they wake. I never am. Hung-over maybe, but sleep-wise you just turn on like a switch. Already having clothes on when you exit your sleeping bag helps skip sleepy morning wake rituals and cut right to the day.

When I describe to people how to find me I tell them my camp is "at that place right before you begin looking." During my first month at Baseline, urges to protect sleep and try and fall back after waking in the middle of the night began to recede. If I woke up at 2am after going to sleep at 10pm I didn't feel as aggravated by the loss of sleep as I would in Status. This easing of the sleep ethic is directly related to how much more alert you are compared to Status. Much less irritated. What was there to do asleep anyway? Weren't tired. No sex dreams. Let's do something.

At dawn's light a few months in you'll pause, stop, feel paralyzed for a moment. Something tugging from a memory. What is that? A list appears, you relax. Bathroom, shower, toilet, toothbrush, holder, cabinet, comb, deodorant, traffic report, weather, email, coffee, breakfast, door, car, tick, tick, tick.

The question "how much time do I have?" grows silent. No alarm clock. You'll freeze in the wind if you shower, walk to the tennis courts to wash. No. You'll just get dirtier afterwards since San Francisco's dampness deposited moisture between your threads. Then you'll sweat when the sun breaks through at noon. Forget it. Nothing calling, everything to call. Nerve wracking?

Negative. Life without time is a beautiful, relaxing feeling.

What I'd do at night is wrap my leather jacket over my backpack to protect electronics content, wear my leather jacket backwards like a straight-jacket to protect it from rain. The jacket also makes an excellent cushion and pillow if I decide to keep my sweater on while I sleep instead of snuggling it beneath my head. My left shoe holds drinks and my speed pipe. My right shoe has my torch, pot pipe, pen, and a key chain with my post office box key and stash tube. I never take my wallet or cell phone out of my drawers.

A small umbrella fits neatly across two branches above me. I can read and work all night using the light of my cell phone display, which is soft enough not to beacon.

Anything round (an apple) tries to roll away from me and down the hill from my inclined abode. It's a comic inconvenience resolved with speed bumps made from tree limbs, and shoes for cup holders. I look for slanted locations when I set up camps in the park. These locations don't attract many Baseliners, who desire flat ground to set up tarps and tents, secure coolers and get bikes up. New arrivals to Baseline, unaware of who sleeps where, often beat resident campers to their spots because the newbies simply get there first. Avoid looking for a new camp at night. You'll want sunlight to examine what you'll be sleeping on. Occupied camps remain empty until very late. Few Baseliners confront newbies in the park if they discover them occupying their camp, unless the old guys are very territorial, have something buried there, are members of the Sf Dogs, or have a very special need for the location (such as a female camper, or cats. (Don't let anyone fool you, dogs can sleep anywhere.)

Unless they want to be heard acting like a jerk, hardly anyone puts up a fight for camp space in the park. If you spot someone in your camp before they're aware of you, it's best to just leave them alone. Oh, and never dart your eyes away from a Baseliner if they make eye contact, at any distance.

Bad form.

Where the fuck did Roy go
with the radio I paid four dollars for?

After half a year snoozing on cement, back pain drove me back the the park. It's nice to be able to have your pick.

I returned to the outskirts of the outdoor roller skate rink between 6th and 7th Avenue, dubbed "the happiest place in Golden Gate Park" by David G. Miles, Jr., the self-proclaimed hardest working man in skating and the rink's weekend MC.

Back pain or not, moving your camp on a regular basis is healthy, rejuvenating, and expected of you by both Baseliners and Status. Besides, we Baseliners are a nomadic bunch and moving makes our life more interesting. You get armloads of help if you can't carry everything in one trip. You get extra stuff if no one needs it, and if you want it. No matter how tired or how busy, unless there's a pressing conflict that involves money, every Baseliner who's capable will drop what they are doing and help you move on the spot. You'll rarely hear "I hate moving" from a Baseliner. It's mostly "guess where I've just been."

In Status, no one's your friend when you're moving.

Outdoors, re-potting yourself in a new camp location helps keep wildlife from depending too much on human routine, allows time for grass to grow back where you slept, reduces permanent hiking and entrance trails, and places regulatory throttles on the number of people who know where you are.

I'd never slept near the roller rink. The location pumps the only tolerated high-volume amplified music in the park, each day from sunrise to dusk.

I wake every morning to Shakuhachi flutes which piper morning exercise and ritual four stories below where I rise from a hill overlooking the rink. A block of blended adult contemporary music signals morning's end and gradually gives way to classic disco and modern house music.

You learn a lot about what music can do to a crowd at Baseline by watching how Status manages music and crowds, be it cocooned people all ear-plugged up, or crowds being forced to leave the park after the 7.46 mile 2014 Bay to Breakers foot race.

After the race MC Miles got an earful from a Park's Department employee who was listening to a voice from a walkie-talkie tell her "no amplified music after 6pm" so MC Miles had to apologize for turning off the disco to over a hundred people settling in to enjoy.

Fun, amplified music is not an effective crowd dispersion tool, which is why all revolutions need a bright, loud theme song to drown out authority.

Any takers out there?

Where's the Baseline revolution song?

I asked Scott Free but he's come up with nothing. Got excited about it though. Yelled at me for not titling this book The Global Homeless Companion. Got so angry his fangs were showing, lips drawn back exposing teeth while he yelled at me. I thought the name was stupid. And the rage Scott showing off for others, demonstrating that he caught me thinking too small. Write a song then.

Man in Black David wished openly he knew how to play the guitar when I asked him where the protest songs are. We're up to our ears in angry music. Then what do we do? All together now: Listen to the protest song.

"There's no music anymore to make anyone want to do anything," Man in Black Dave lamented with me one evening on Hippy Hill. It was right after Oyster Fest so the sprawling lawn below was littered with trash, scavengers, and a few booths still breaking down,

"No good protest songs," Man in Black Dave repeated. "No protest songs at all, not even bad ones."

"How can you have a bad protest song? That's like selecting a bad national anthem. A depressing wedding song."

"Sure, lots of pissed off songs but no group protest numbers. Did I say that right? Nothing to organize around. Nothing that talks to all different types of people," Man in Black Dave said, handing me a polished metal pill bottle with a screw top and key chain. These were water proof and popular among speed dealers holding a warehouse.

"Here, you can have this," Bird said. "I found a whole rack of them."

I had some pot to stash in it that Ziggy gave me, took it.

"Why is that?' I asked about the music.

Man in Black Dave coughed, covering his mouth with the right sleeve of his black dinner jacket. He though about something.

"As a kid I remember my Mom rolling down a window when she was driving alone, lighting one of Dad's cigarettes, turning up the radio and humming along with Buffalo Springfield," he laughed. "Come to think of it we didn't write any protest songs. Our parents did."

Drugs

From your first taste of sugar to your last drip of morphine you have always enjoyed drugs, and always will.

A friend of high respect during my freshman year who, for while, sent pound containers of freeze dried psychedelic mushrooms to me FedEx overnight from the college he'd transferred to, would routinely question the nature of man's appetite for narcotics. He considered the habits of all the great thinkers, artists, creative minds for good and evil, and suggested man is ultimately drawn to oblivion. His word, not mine, which is why it stuck.

Let's be clear: Under any condition, Baseline is a party, a celebration of life at first touch. Baseline festivities overshadow selfish positions and absorbed attitudes imported with new arrivals. Your maiden euphoria at Baseline can be sustained indefinitely if you wish. And taken way over factory specifications if that is what you are looking for. At Baseline you are free.

Free from time and calendaring. You never have to leave a moment. If party up high is the way you fly, never kiss that scene goodbye.

A good example of this is the fact that Baseline is one of the few places left in the world where you can get compensation for poetry written in English. That's supposed to be uplifting.

Do all the drugs you want at Baseline. No one will notice. No one will care. There are no rules. "No rules" prevents failure. Failure is a loss. What kind of society are we, again?

As I type in these notes, I have just run out of speed and money for alcohol. I have a lot of pot. Everyone does. Baseline is swimming right now in free, nearly tasteless weed as trim dumps in from Northern California.

Trimmers get free trim to take with them along with a salary after making sure a grower's wares get to market before molding.

Trim is cool. You can make a menu of cannabis candies out of trim. Hash oil, pot butter for baking, hand cream for joint pain, stiff doobies that run. Trouble is, Trim looks like green sand. No domestic middle-class Status dealer would ever sell trim unless there was nothing else under the sun.

An enormous amount of trim finds its way to market fenced as currency for speed dealers. The speed dealers mostly give it away to people they know who don't do alot of speed. That group cooks hash oil with it and trades it for anything. Food, clothes, jewelry. The next tier down tries to smoke it, rolling it with tobacco for a more consistent burn. What's left or become uninteresting is thrown away only to be found in a dumpster dive. Then the cycle repeats itself starting with the Tweekers.

So my pot right now (an ounce of trim) is slightly more valuable than a container of tap water. Trim needs to come in pounds before it has any negotiable value. What I have wouldn't load a pipe if I cooked it down.

As I type in these notes, I have just run out of speed and money for alcohol.

Addiction is primarily a habit of inventory mentality. Baseline, and only Baseline allows you to demonstrate this to yourself.

I have no beer on me. If I'd just finished my last beer, back in my old apartment on Potrero Hill, I wouldn't be typing this sentence right now. I'd be having a fit, counting pennies, figuring out how to get another beer, and keep them coming. How not to get sick, feel like throwing up. I'd begin feeling that way when I opened that last beer, knowing it was the last and not wanting to forget it. I was "sick" in Status. But no more.

Why? Inventory mentality. Typical of our refusal to accept loss. The code planted in our social algorithms that got everything around us built has its fingerprints all over this. You don't want the beer, you don't want a cigarette, you don't need to get high. Sure it feels great but it's that you don't want to run out of it. Unbearable. It's a task, keep going until WE say stop.

Here's why the stomach turns in sick withdrawal thirst not when you've finished the last bottle off, but as you open the last bottle. Like the second half of a presidential term is devoted primarily to getting reelected, that last bottle, joint, whatever, will not be about enjoying it. It will be about re-upping, getting another, do it while you still have some left. Inventory mentality. How do you beat this?

Painful, prolonged withdrawal therapies like those described in the book *Drunkard* by Neil Steinberg provide plenty of excuses for relapsing into addition, or drowning out the world with a bottle. Steinberg's lived this and writes that withdrawing alcoholics should be dropped into deep forests with only a match and a dull knife to survive, rather than trapped within four white walls which drove them to drink in the first place.

There are Baseliners who say they are addicts all the time and tell you the drug because A) they want to get to the drug as soon as possible and don't care what you think if you don't have a roll in the hunt, or B) they've attended so many AA meetings they think their drug of choice is their last name.

There really are no addicts at Baseline. Baseliners aren't that single-minded. The ones who nonchalantly say they are addicts are deaf to the negative impact a drug reference can have on even the simplest sentence.

"We'll, I'm gonna go see if I can drum up some money so I can get high."

These are victims of too many programs that encourage banal drug speak as if it might lend more self-awareness. It only serves to display a one-track mind, and not the one that should be on display. I think about feeling high and getting stoned and having orgasms all the time, through every sentence. It's called looking forward to recreation. I just don't make recreation the subject of every sentence.

Welfare has the option to categorize Baseliners as addicts. So do homeless support groups in order to satisfy reimbursement requirements from State and Federal fund matching programs that prime their services.

Baseliners can cry addiction in order to keep a welfare check coming, or increase their monthly payment. But they are full of. Classic addiction behavior doesn't apply at Baseline. The sickness doesn't work. Withdrawal pain doesn't stick, it wears off almost instantly then settles back like a memory. You can't close off input at Baseline. Even alone, there is no place to hide. The high radiance of cerebral input from Dense Now overwhelms the anxiety of loss. It is 'that loss' an addict feels, having nothing to do but inventory control in the time preserves of Status.

Like the Candy Rack, a typical house in Status contains confined spaces and time-capture mechanisms that can provide many choices, but no factory installed choice for stopping anything. The choices are also incentives to "get back to times like those pictured". No stop button. Maybe a stashed beer in the crisper. I'd have to check.

Status, overclocked and over inventoried and scrutinized by expectations and memories is simply the wrong soil for conclusiveness. Status provides no comfortable stopping point for excessive drug or alcohol use.

Status cannot offer a good choice to who likes drugs and drink.

"You've got to go to work in the morning" isn't a choice whether or not to stop doing a drug. It's a set of choices for deciding how to keep going: Go in smelling like pot, call in sick, work from home, go in and avoid customers, leave early, struggle until 5pm. How do you sober up with a drum beat of shame from hypocrites disobeying their own higher standards compound the pain with a fear shot and a panic chaser?

At Dense Now my first notes detailed my loss of appetite for consuming anything. Liberation from time liberates from addiction. Laboratory mice within four walls live and die showing signs of addiction. There are no mice addicts running around Baseline. Not even the rats with their own labs.

There is no one and nothing at Baseline to remind you that a drug is in your system.

In the exact opposite, Status is blanketed by 1st time user anti-drug propaganda, sobriety cheerleaders rooting for carnal worship, and an ingenious paranoia mechanism that is going to take time to correct in the game of life at its highest level. In Status, endless warnings pose the silent paranoid question at every juncture: Will People Know?

Pot, weed, nuggets, herb, ganja, buds, grass, marijuana, the stickiest of the icky. Thank our maker Mother Earth for this perfect drug. Pot is nature's every-man drug. Smoke a fatty in a healthy mental state and witness humanity's Sun shine in.

What? Who the fuck is that? Made you feel all "I gotta get outta here" paranoid the first time? That's a feature of a good pot buzz, not a failing of the weed. Mmmmh, now that' good paranoia. There is a difference.

Artificial people trigger paranoia. Example, cops.

Paranoia is pot's way of prompting you to scream

"What the hell is all this dangerous man-made nonsense doing around me?" To that end, pot awakens within you your own special warrior for the freeing of the natural humanity of others which is never an armed conflict.

This means pot is no industry drug. No sir. Pot didn't make the meeting when all those scary types were in the room. Ask too much of pot and it dies. You cannot promise a "next year's model".

You can only get so high from pot, but you can be absolutely satisfied with it, even though this peak experience only lasts so long (see the song Crackling Rose by Neil Diamond)

Pot is not a vehicle drug. You can only smoke so much pot before you reach a ceiling of maximum stoned. After that point all pot consumption is a habitual waste, or you are on acid and don't care.

Smart drug, that marijuana. Smart Earth.

Remember What Drug You're On

"Hey Man, Why You Doing
Mad Drugs Outside of the Library?"

Speed, meth, coke, milk, crank, powder, product, go-fast, Sandra Bullock's first feature film, whatever you're crew wants you to call it, speed reinforces the humanity within you, not necessarily other people's humanity (Hint: as other people are likely going to be afraid to tell you). Pot is absolutely satisfying. Speed is absolutely dissatisfying.

Totally dissatisfying. Which is why it's such a kick ass drug to use when you want to completely break away from the gravitational pull of feeling the least bit sorry for your actions. You witness Status for what it currently is, a restrictive compression chamber state our outmoded thinking continues to build as if still beneath whip and ration. You see the code that needs to be patched when you do Meth. Imagination? Try it.

That's what speed does, so it makes sense that speed is a synthetic and not an organic product of nature. Speed gets along with everyone, but speed is only about you, and it's cheap, looks like pot smoke, has a ridiculously long lasting buzz, and is alien.

Charming up ones humanity too often with speed can bear larger than life consequences. This is why the Baseline dividends speed can pay often backfire when the drug is administered in Status. Speed working away in a person whose dissatisfied persona is propped up by lies and prematurely realized ambition can create a monster, and this change can take place in both Status and Baseline.

It's particularly dangerous in Status. A monster knows only what it wants and disregards anything that stands in its way. There is a monster in every trap.

"Do you know where to find any speed?"
"Sure, follow the sound of fighting."

Drugs, like food, have their table manners which people have the option to notice when missing. Most mannerisms revolve around conserving the drug, and making sure everyone in the circle is afforded equal share of it. There are few big no-nos here.

Take for example "Abandon Submarine". It's the look you don't want to see on the person you are sharing your speed with. It's that squishy face caused by a person sucking in as much speed through a piezo pipe and into their lungs as possible, as if their life depended on it.

That "one hit" they begged you for and said they'll get you back for whenever they can could end up weighing half your shit. This tasteless and obvious fiending of the drug shows zero self-control, especially if their eyes roll back cross-eyed in their head.

It's blatantly greedy and debasing.

Submarine duty Tweekers like Mayor McTweek and Hawaii 5-0 check their dignity at the screen door when they pull this stunt, which explains their strange brag that they can "take a punch." The drug is now your conscious and you are no longer conscious of the drug. This generally gives you two routes going forward:

A) Apologize to a lot of people, or proceed as normal and state your behavior as version 2.0 or

B) Be your speedy self. Both actions are welcome, chosen lifestyles at Baseline. Show up the same guy every time.

Speed switches off your time-based prohibitors, which is why you experience a perfect world platform from speed, which speed does not want to let you know. You know you're high, you are unbridled in all directions. You are freed from time. Anything-goes possibilities you locked away fearing the consequences are set free to roam, without conscience. Fear is totally stripped away. The application is not crime alone, nowhere near it. Anyone who harbors such an idea should be politely asked to try it. Thinking the drug won't kill you is a crime.

What I find to be the highest value of speed but also the most lethal is when the time based prohibitors finally switches off. They do not get switched back on. Your conscious is now the shepherd of a much larger flock of desires and opportunities. The fastest way to address this is to do more speed. Speed puts you in charge. So if there's anything hanging you up, that's the distance you could go down. You won't regret anything. Anything. But you did it.

Tweekers can't seem to escape coming across as if they only care about consuming speed. They do not care about you. Like you? Sure. And that sucks. Any Baseliner can come up to me and say "Man, I'd love a drag of that," I'll smoke all I can with them if they are partying with me, and not the drug.

Real conversations are just that, real. Reciprocating. "Thanks again man. My food stamps are on the ninth and I can feed you then if you need anything, anything you want. "

A Siphoner will say, if the subject of money arises, that he has two houses in Hawaii.

"No I don't drink or smoke pot. I just do speed" is another heavy Siphoner warning sign unless they are dealers.

If a Tweeker starts to follow me saying "hey I'm going that way too" then notice he begins to make every turn I make, no matter which way I'm going or were headed, I start to rub their bad manner back into them. I want and see how long this human being can operate on absolute zero dignity. So I'll keep walking, sometimes taking my speed pipe out and looking at it before ignoring his request to "step into these bushes and lite that up."

I'll say "nah" and head to Safeway. Twenty minutes of shopping for lunch on food stamps and he'll be waiting outside, though I didn't ask. Just said bye. Then he'll nicely tail me to the roller rink where I sit to eat. He isn't hungry I learn, still hanging around. Fiendishly certain that no matter what, yes, no matter what, soon, I'll want to smoke the speed. Soon. And he'll be there. He knows I have some. And he'll be there. I finish eating as the guy rattles off places "we" can go so he can charge his smart phone, places like Starbucks which is right up there.

"You struck me the as the Starbucks type," he says.

He's been told for the last two hours that charging batteries is what I do at the library while I work. Instead of passing out beneath a tree waiting for the evening distribution to arrive to the crews.

"Really, you seemed like a Starbucks guy to me."

I pick up my lunch waste and put my back pack on. "Take care bro. It was great chatting with you." A radiate not a drop of animosity or hurry.

"Hey, can we do one more round on the pipe?"

Walk away.

These scenes always leaves me feeling disgusted by the one thing I fear: Loss of control of the self.

The next morning I'm sitting with Harriett and Hawaii 5-0, the man with two houses in Hawaii, walked up looking like anyone's proud beautiful day in Golden Gate Park. He sat next to me on Harriet's blanket and Queenie-Bee exposed her gums.

"You wanna split a bag?" he whispered loud enough for Harriett to hear him.

"No."

His expression was a gasp. Surprise comedy. Seriously.

The "no" shook him up so bad he wound the E-string on Harriet's guitar so tightly that it broke with a twang. He'd been trying to tune it when I turned him down. It wasn't the money, I could tell. He imagined some deeper relationship with me than wasn't there.

There is no penalty for the word "no" in Baseline. Where people can accept final and conclusive loss.

The American Homeless Companion is challenging Methamphetamine's claim to be any such thing as speed.

It is not.

It is a hallucinogenic.

And thus, *The American Homeless Companion* has the position that Speed is Not Addictive.

In its effect, the removal of time-based prohibitors is exhilarating. Once removed any avenue is open, and can be visualized with astonishing detail. Success relies on you radiating yourself outwards, and not getting trapped in other people's nightmares, an inward action.

Speed's popularity is the measure of our society's dearth of satisfying things to do. A choice is to dream those things, become, then radiate outwards, the world an extension of yourself at all times.

Be careful.

Apocalyptic Language

"My God, the genius of that, the genius, the will to do that. Perfect, genuine, complete, crystalline, pure. And then I realized they could stand that--these were not monsters, these were men, trained cadres, these men who fought with their hearts, who have families, who have children, who are filled with love--that they had this strength, the strength to do that. If I had ten divisions of those men, then our troubles here would be over very quickly."

We misuse language so severely that not only are deep layers of information received with a word not recognized or illuminated by the context of their use, but also those delivering a word in speech or media may not realize the collective instruction of the word, or that it delivers more information than intended.

Look how much information about Colonel Kurtz's attack strategy is revealed when he utters the word "divisions."

Casual listeners – all of us – hear a quantity. A number. Our take away is Kurtz has gone mad and wants an impossible number of soldiers to follow through with his plan.

What is not heard except by military personnel and those who looked the word "division" up is that Kurtz's plan requires 10 battle fronts. A single army divided to attack 10 separate points of weakness. That's very specific information that Martin Sheen's commanders, aware of their weaknesses on all fronts, could have easily used to foil Kurtz if the machete hacking doesn't go as planned. But we don't hear a voice-over of Martin Sheen saying to himself "So that was his plan. Far from a suicide mission. Hoa Ben, Quy Nhon, Vihn Long... home to Hanoi. Shit." Kurtz's resume, detailed in an earlier scene in the movie, would not merit the misuse of the word "division." If you used the word "division" casually to Kurtz he would get more information than you likely intended, and he would act in a way you did not realize you triggered.

Now, writer Francis Ford Coppola either thought about this military language and researched it, or he got lucky, which is equally disturbing because subliminal suggestion using deep definition words and language work the same way.

Atop this, words and phrases part of our common language enshrined by real acts of human and societal courage - words that free people - have been relegated to people's imaginations. Peace. Sacrifice. Resistance.

We use a diction of fun house mirror terms knowing full well a clear picture is not being articulated, that we are in fact lying, if only by distortion of detail.

The American Homeless Companion understands: It is extraordinarily difficult to see our society behaving this way, as it truly is, as we made it to operate and have left it running, unless you break from the model that supports it.

How We Got To Where We Are,
and Why it's Nobody's Fault

We are a people at war with ourselves.

It is not how anyone ever wanted it to be. It is not a conspiracy. No person is at fault, no matter how rich or how poor. Ending this war with ourselves begins with recognition that there is no enemy. There is no aggressor, so no need to fear vulnerability or loss. Our war with ourselves can end when we depart from a narrow set of choices that require products to fill gaps in satisfaction and display, and present ourselves with a wider, unlimited set off choices.

There are many ways to conduct warfare.

Philosopher Paul Virilio in his book Pure War terrifies your sense of control when you can no longer disagree that the U.S government wages war on Africa when it fails to send needed AIDS drugs, essentially a war against poor African people. The same can be said about the locations an American can have a safe but spotty allowance of abortions, which appears to be a woman's rights issue battling religion's hold on sanctity of life but in reality has been getting better returns as the backdoor to the willful self-extermination of liberals, who have the most abortions and have voter concentration in liberal cities with electorally powerful states that indoctrinate equally liberal children. A society that can accept loss would immediately recognize abortion geography as a war on liberals via their own self-inflicted reduction in numbers.

If you blame Baseliners and want them and their way of life gone, then you are war with the homeless. If you have imagined someway to sympathize with Baseliners, but agree they should stand silent as they are meaninglessly ticketed... Then you are at war.

When Americans and the world deny people their natural human rights to basic God-given essentials the Earth has provided such as free whole foods (apples, oranges, wheat, corn, etc.) and space to dwell – not a house or apartment but a free space to dwell anywhere someone else is not – America, and the world, is at war with its people.

The so-called homeless - our only live, public human display of social loss – are allowed to remain visible in measure to keep working people working and all others at a terror level of dependence.

Like other forms of soft-weapon, homelessness' polarizing effect on people has been institutionalized in order to achieve the larger political goal of slave reinforcement.

Now remember, there is no enemy to point a finger at in this war. No outside slave master to attack when the word slave is mentioned. There is no aggressor.

Wars are decisions that are made. Bad decisions result all the time from a lack of good choices. A few seemingly minor errors in mankind's thinking since the dawn of our society continues to contaminate our choices no matter how smart we think we are. These errors, which reside in the way we see ourselves and subvert our own prowess, have been overlooked because they reside in our humbleness, in our hearts, which we resist investigating or condemning. Exposed or not, our heart is our benchmark of decency. Mess with its purity and we lose our way home.

So political and social changes have always arrived with accusations aimed at people who don't share the heart of the revolutionaries. Begging the question of why should anyone care about shared hearts when the revolution is unstoppable, regardless of who supports it?

"Oh, but we simply must find a way to accommodate

both sides of an argument. Why would you square off two commentators against each others opinion of a certain law when the act the law applies to is unconstitutional? The opposing argument is meaningless hot air either waiting for Congress to come back in session or baiting people to righteously break the law. Arguing a side as if it's actively debatable. Nonsense. But veneer of a news program sells it to people as if it is such.

This is mankind lying to itself. Trying to cast blame. No side in any man-made conflict has ever been at fault for their station in life. What they do, who they are, how much they own or don't. Each person involved was where they were because of the decisions they made in life, one by one, minute by minute. If they were deemed corrupt, it was because their choices were corrupt. Here is where the age old minor errors we made may reside. Here we begin to see that it's the staggeringly long list of stuff we've created, argued over, and imagined that's been the catalyst of bad choices. Man-man non-realities, instead of our own present-time wisdom, took over the helm of choice selection. We look to things and creations as more suited to offer and become the choices we have. It's easier that way, as the choices delivered mostly deliver the preservation of things and ways, turning a cheek to the potential collateral damage real-time, significant change can bring. A society that cannot accept loss.

Slavery was not abolished. It was promoted. The masters are us.

In so many works of fiction, our future slave masters are stuff we built. A nemesis composed of lots of great ideas for all sorts of tools that collectively, as a single tool, turned out to be a bad idea that – it goes without saying – no one saw coming.

How come?

Probably because as each of the man-made tools making up the future slave master were introduced separately, and sometimes years apart, each creation - at any point in history - was a celebration for people. We'd discovered something new. How could anyone see the slave master coming when every step along the way to its assembly was a celebration? An invention here, a new discovery there with no evidence that engineering inflatable rubber would many years later help another idea – cars - flourish to the demise of Earth's environment, or that certain chemicals created to preserve stuff or make stuff appear more attractive might cause health problems. Anyone with an unsettling vision of a new discovery or invention at its onset would be told to relax and have some Campaign.

"Here's to progress, everyone! We're going to win an award for this one!"

There are so many other examples but the bottom line is that as industry churned away, any hint that something bad, something that might not make people all that satisfied was popularly ignored, and for a very logical reason.

No one had a blueprint for everything we see around us that is man-made. There was no industry on Earth before the arrival of mankind's idea of industry. No plan or end destination to steer our industrial progress towards. No manufacturing system that succeeded or failed before the thought of mass production came to us in our infancy. No precedent. No one showed up at the invention of product replication and said "Hey guys, we tried this back with the dinosaurs and it really bummed people out after a while."

There was indeed a plan for each new product industry produced: A house, a car, a fashion accessory. All were nifty thoughts for specific uses. But people like you and I hatched those plans. Not industry, which is a man-made idea.

You cannot do anything with industry, the same way you cannot wear knitting, which is also an idea. You can wear a knit sweater and build a house with an industrial strength hammer, but ideas and what they create are always separate, and if an idea that is creating something has no precedent, nothing before it as a guide, then not even the smartest person has any exact idea of what the end results of the idea will eventually look like, or when to hit the stop button if they feel things have turned for the worse.

How could the stop button have ever been hit?

When Elvis Presley, The King of Rock and Roll, killed himself by consuming too much of everything over a span of decades there was no precedent for Elvis. No Elvis that came before our culture's Elvis that would have prompted Mr. Presley's loved ones, friends and investors to whisper into The King's ear "Hey Elvis, you have to cool it man. If you keep popping all those pills and eating like you are you are going to pull an Elvis."

We know Elvis didn't listen. The look he got from his bodyguards, handlers and flunkies was clearly one of worship and dependence. Just watch the old reels. In his barber chair in Graceland's master bathroom Elvis certainly must have reflected on this close group's advice to take better care of himself, but what level of respect he had for them and their opinions no one really knows. Elvis was likely as bedazzled by his own success as anyone and had plainly never seen an example of over-consumption at an unbridled rate that led to anything worse than the need to go on a diet. There's an "act as if" expression on his face in the last images of Elvis, bloated and sweating as he sang, handed one towel after the other turning the perspiration of an eroding body into fan memorabilia. He wasn't going to flinch. If he was fat as a pig, he was still on top, he was still Elvis. No one needed, or really wanted to see his gray underbelly.

So the King of Rock and Roll, intimidating and admired,

the first of his kind, wealthy and popular, unquestioned, did just what he wanted to do, giving musicians forever after him a life-saving anecdote on avoiding self-destruction in a hedonistic industry.

American industrial society is an "Elvis" in many ways. Without precedent, intimidating in its growth, admired by us, unquestioned when it comes to the tough stuff. Our industrial society, founded in part for private property ownership rights, also has a side of it that most of us know about but prefer not to discuss or even recognize. The word homeless tells you all you need to know so you can marginalize the condition, direct out-flowing anger and frustration, and dismiss industry's role from your attention.

Homeless. Industry save us. I one of a thing doesn't save us how could a hundred replicas? What are we doing with one if they've had one for months and are still arguing next door? Who wanted it? You? Or Industry, or as a bridge to communicate like interests to other people?,

A house is a product. Like a toy is a product. Industry itself, a product. A home is the same as a house. No difference. The word home is just as divisive as homeless, the word's nostalgic echo of protective family tradition tugging our hearts all sappy about Normal Rockwell family lives many of us never had in the first place. This is how you make products appear to be necessities. Captains of industry want to see all of their product experiments become mainstays.

People work for necessities. They save for luxuries. Here's a key to how this ratio has checks and balances on it:

There is no such thing as a man-made necessity.

People distanced from the natural food cycle don't work.

Work is not progress. Progress is not work.

Imposed order always forcibly disrupts.

Decisions not to die always fail.

Composure inflates.

Only purchase $5 worth of any drug at a time, always.
Never sleep without attaching your backpack and other.
belongings to your body.
Never front money to anyone.
Never loan chargers, phones or PCs to anyone.
Carry and possess as few things as possible.
When Departing Status, Depart Status Symbols.

The Great Unspoken –
Park Meth is a Sex Fantasy Drug

"Man I'm not afraid to say anything that's the truth. I already masturbated twelve times because speed is such a visual drug."

- Mayor McTweek, May, 2014

Speed is not addictive. Meth is not addictive. That is all bullshit.

The lazy assumption that meth or speed is dangerously addictive arrives as a scarecrow planted to spook people away from a potentially good choice that's not in the rule book. Speed use is a better choice than lots of other choices (millions) that fall way short of what's expected of them. Psychology, coffee, muscle stiffness, libido, sleep aides. Yes, like a baby, when you want.

I list libido but I can hardly get it up on speed. And I feel like its throwing odd signals at my prostate. I get backed up when I try to pee on the drug. So I've stopped trying to rub one out on speed and concentrate instead on visuals. Fantasy sex is where my head is at when the speed shows up.

I know several Status men and women who venture out to Buena Vista Park to score speed and skedaddle and you can see it written all over their faces in their urgency. They aren't paranoid and want to split, they want to get home and play with themselves.

The American Homeless Companion strongly endorses Meth as a sex drug.

Do not contact family members when using it.

The American Homeless Companion wholeheartedly endorses and supports masturbation of all kinds.

It's your body. Use it or lose it.

Never let them see you sweat

As language's responsibility to truth and numerical equivalency wane, images become increasingly relied upon to decide on choices we are given, less than words. Added reliance on images in decision making accelerates the process. We see images as more honest. Words can now deceive without lying.

Words are for the body. Our minds record everything which includes images. It's the decision maker. Words have become more for our body, commands after a decision is made, for example. The "stops" and "goes" the mind won't obey, and doesn't have to. The body obeys. The steady retreat by words from their numerical equivalents (whatever the scale used - time, urgency, heat, value) has played havoc on our bodies stress engines. We know less what to prepare for. We hear "jump" (a word) and the question is how high? There is no fixed math to "jump". Could be high, low. Center would be the most intelligent reaction. The word "decade" has fixed numerical calibration, 10 years. But the word flies by in a sentence spoken loosely and registers as a generality "very long time".

"This vintage is aged over a decade, it says here. France."

That's shitty wine. But it aged right in your hand.

So your body stands at attention waiting for words from you. Their commands, up to the body, not necessarily the mind, which is designed (designed, not always operated) to be honest and accurate in all communication except action, which the body has the most say in.

The arrival of Natural Providership as a shoring mechanism for Baseliners Greatly reduces that "at attention" feeling that overworks the body which has instinct

to do, to act, stay forever ready. As you near Dense Now, the separation between you and your body increases exponentially with the proximity to the state of absolute present. This is best compared to the Status state of unconscious action, blacking out, or hypnosis, each of which are Status states of time abandonment, seeking productivity through subtraction versus addition (i.e., the thoughtless but safe navigation of the last few paces towards your dwelling when your mind has dropped the reins.)

At Baseline, as you near Dense Now, this is your body awakening to its free will, which is really your body's own separate and trusted network of following through and completing behaviors, acting out your chosen strategic goals while your mind is free to ponder something else.

Meet your second self. Your body's free will, operating along a secondary path from your brain to perform and rectify chores and complications. This is Natural Providership under full employment. Your second self begins to cast its own shadow about six months into Baseline, and at first, it will scare the hell out of you.

At this early level of maturity as a Baseliner, tasks you

assign yourself within any real time frame get done without you worrying about it, even if you think you are worrying about it. Think about that one. Read this slowly: If you are worried about getting your laundry done before heading back to the library, and you engage in this worry while what appears before you is your body, another one, taking clothes from a washer and placing them in a dryer, your second body would probably notice you and laugh, asking "don't you have anything better to do with your time than to worry about me?"

I remember the first time I watched my body, from a distance, from my camp, walk with my clean and folded clothes towards me where I sat jotting down notes for an oncology feature assignment. I never looked happier in my life. I did appear to be in something of a trance though. It wasn't pure imagination, me about fifteen feet away from me, doing laundry. It was a projection using imagination's equipment to image. I've never seen anything clearer in my life. Or more lonely.

Why haven't we let our bodies off the hook? Or allow our mind to think we had to baby sit our body all the time? Watch every move.

How often we see virtuoso's perform without paying any attention to their dexterity. Why do we watch our hands and pay attention to each finger's movement during so many ordinary functions? Did our minds become bored, or were we not given or allowed enough to do?

Consider how much more you could get accomplished if you truly trusted your body (not yourself) and let your body take care of things you've ordered yourself to do, accomplished without supervision. Remember, it's still you, and you're one physical presence to onlookers. This is how you appear to you after a while at Baseline.

Consider how little physical pain we'd have to endure if we relied on second self to endure pain without engaging the mind. Who said our high-level thinking and emotional expressions had to ride sidesaddle with the painful pulsing of a torn hangnail? Or a stinging wound, or the belt of withdrawal? Enough. There's a way to know it's there without feeling pain. We're way over the need for that cattle prod. No shit, I need a band aid, a doctor. I know, I looked, the pains not going to make anything happen any faster.

But for centuries the pain did need to be sent. To get everything you see around that's man-made, built and running. It can stand down now. Allow it to through the realization and use of second self.

What would be the body's resting dream of the mind?

"Trust yourself."

A very wise person got that saying into everyday conversation some time ago, but we have fallen short of understanding its profoundness. It suggests a separation, an action from one thing to another. But that thoughtful deconstruction has been dumbed down to marching orders printed on lunch room posters showing cats clinging to life (thank you, erosion of words).

In Status, this separation is winked at, but never taken under control. "I did that all by myself."

"Hey, I know you are impatient to get this done, but slow down. Take care of yourself will ya? You're gonna wear yourself out."

"Take care of my what?" you might ask yourself.

The phrase "it's important to take care of your body" is a cosmetics industry lure at all levels of Status that omits the self, considering only the body as a canvas for its many applications.

Take care of yourself is an order sent from body to mind. The body has to ask. It has no power over the mind, although it can cause pain. The mind is all powerful over the body, and will catch mistakes the body makes. The mind can kill the body. Not the other way.

Homeless Notice

Don't Hide Your Head in Your Hands and Act Like You Suck....

There is no "Scarp" in the current state of homelessness.

You are a beggar or you provide value and entertain.

You beg by being honest. Ask for what you need, don't lie.

You entertain or provide your natural value, like fixing things or selling drugs.

Beggars suck, and are depressing.

No one has the right to make anyone feel uncomfortable.

Entertaining people rule, make more money, and have more fun.

And by the way, how can begging be gratifying? Sitting on a cold concrete sidewalk with your head in your hands? Some cardboard sign asking for anything. What are you thinking when you are down there? What's going through your mind when you are not looking at the beauty all around you? Or even just talking to people?

Are you thinking: "Oh things suck, and suck, suck, suck, suck, suck..."

Or perhaps this: "If this bitch buy a slice for me instead of giving me the money I'll shit."

When you laugh the world laughs with you. When you cry, you cry alone.

Homeless

Kelly Joy Grabianowski

Displaced urgency
Unstable angst
Ungrounded fear
I close my eyes to be met by those of a cougar, lae round
golden flames captivating my whole being
She is searching. Alone. Wandering.
I see leopards and lions and tigers elephants
humming birds
great apes
trees all fallen
Miss placed
Displaced
Homeless
All feeling the depleting
Feeling the broken
More and more people
Less and less space
Land
Homes
The depth of homelessness
continues to unfold to me
The irony of a panther pacing in his cage
Ripped from his forest that no longer exists
Preservation has its cost
Displaced.
Like a zoo in reverse
Pacing
I feel they are frantic
I feel their sorrow
I feel now what it means to have no place
No place to go home to
This growing enveloping knowing

Trauma
Expanding homelessness as we kill and cut and destroy each other
as we kill our mother
We kill ourselves
Where can we go?
Where can we go to cure our desire to self destruct
Where can we go to show such deep sorrow
rage
How can we continue to lose so much and gain so little?
I close my eyes to see tree roots grounding deeper, trunks and branches reaching above, breathing and screaming for change, for ground in which to create community in.
I see lines of lost souls marching to nowhere
Thousands more displaced
Feeling the weight of lifetimes carried on tired backs
Not knowing where home will exist again
My eyes follow seeds and fruits as they fall upon concrete
Generations lost at the price of "civilization"
Until they land heavily back into the pleading eyes of mountain lions demanding that I wake up
That I dare to look around me with an open heart, broken, bleeding, feeling.
I answer back with tears and unspoken promises.

Electric Loser Land

Good Job. Now stop

Look around you. If this were Rome we'd all agree that the aqueducts are built, so to speak. Good job. We've finished making pretty much all we need and know how to make. So where are our choices to enjoy all that we've made? Where is the above board decision to say stop.

All this great stuff we have? The ease in which we live isn't being realized? Is being treated like we're doing it all for someone else to mess with, not us.

And now we have a surplus a people. People degraded as "homeless" but who *The American Homeless Companion* recognizes as the occupants of Baseline, a new economic layer just below poverty. Born from a successful, peaceful society free of famine, plague, poor drinking water, cataclysmic infrastructure failures. Allowing us to run up the head count by preventing loss.

Baseliners. The surplus results from humanity's success, not short comings.

If you and I operated a commercial orange grove and we had a surplus of oranges this season we'd celebrate. Lots of extra oranges to sell and we didn't have to spend a dime extra on fertilizer, manpower, or any other expense we budgeted for. But we got lots and lots of extra oranges to sell. Looks like we're going to make a profit.

Why so glum about a surplus of people? Shouldn't this be fantastic news? People that really place no drag on society by doing nothing? They may look like shit, lack basic dignity, try and steal everything you own, and terrify you into putting up with the worst job you have ever had to endure, but the concentration and community of homeless people who have formed what Baseline is today are the key to you never having to worry about your job or your security ever again.

Excellent, right?

Finally, we don't live in a society screaming for more people to grab a pail and carry water. We have people leaning on shovels. Jealous? Stop working.

This is the dawning of the Age of People Who Simply Have Nothing to Do. The ranks of the employed already bubble over with people who don't want to do anything at all. Why not let these people stop working if they don't want to work? You may be one of them.

Wouldn't allowing people who don't care about working to leave the workforce, thereby improving the quality of all products and services? Reducing competition against those who really long to do the work, instead of have to?

Wouldn't it part the clouds for those who really care and really have an ambition to accomplish their goals without unnecessarily competing against sub-par workers who will be happy to tell you they're only around because they need the job to pay rent and eat?

Couldn't we stop then and ask ourselves why we continue to churn out unnecessary garbage just to keep from cutting people's hours? People who would love to work less, if given the option.

We have succeeded as a society. We got our caveman asses off the ground and got a lot of great ideas built. We're rich. You just haven't unwrapped it yet.

Now it is time to stop mandatory enlistment in the work force.

Now is the time for Baseline Economics.

When you remove yourself from the man-made constraints of time and calendaring, when you enter Baseline, experience Natural Providership, observe Dense Now, you will see how we are all innocent of getting caught in the repeating cycle of industry that had to be programmed into us to get anything done. The introspection that *The American Homeless Companion* operates from is called root cause analysis. A tiny algorithm in our collective code needs to be updated, a line of command that slants our decision making. A line that reads "We cannot accept loss". A line that must be updated to "Accept loss forever".

Status, you must embrace what you do not know.

Every Baseliner knows how to fold a sheet, clean a kitchen, lock a door, make a bed, order movies on demand and listen to the wind whistle against the windows.

Do you know how to secure a safe camp in Golden Gate Park, where it's technically illegal to sleep? Find a shadowy, peaceful spot beneath the stars where you can get that three hours of sleep you pay thousands of dollars a month for in Status? Do you know how to stay fed and healthy without digging through garbage cans for food?

The American Homeless Companion calls on Status to experience Baseline. It calls on Baseliners to accept and be proud of their station at Baseline. It calls on all people to rejoice that there is a new room we can play in, an expansion of our socioeconomic ladder which ends second-class citizenship at Baseline. Which is testament to our success.

You can stop now if you want. It's okay.

Today is Columbus Day, 2014.

Who made up the crew ledgers of The Nina, The Pinto and The Santa Maria? The ships of Columbus's fleet? Who were these sailors and passengers and Indian slaughterers homesteading new frontier and representing a surplus of people generated by their own successful, empirical society back home?

Who were they? They were the losers, the drunks, the fuckups and criminals, the cast-offs, crazies, shit bags. People who no one cared about being swallowed up by sea monsters. Royalty of any kind was not on-board these explorer crafts. Well, maybe that one special royal family member, you know which one.

The American Homeless Companion asks: What has changed about our expectations of the first people to settle and populate a paradise?

Baseliners, the people who the world will soon know and recognize as the original inhabitants of America's first free society, the world's end destination of human and civil rights, are supposed to be. Tough motherfuckers who can demonstrate by action that There is No Such Thing as a man-made Necessity.

You.

Now.

Our Bad, Nasty Habit of Calling Things False

Stuff

I began to collect stuff at Baseline in my first few weeks here, but gave up on it. I could not find the convenience in having stuff, products laying around doing nothing but getting relocated. If I needed tweezers or tape, I'd ask for it when I had the time to use it. No planning ahead.

In Status, if you want to make a video and break out the idea in front of friends or particularly loved ones, you'll likely be ignored and warned about something tactical that people look for to fail, such as "you don't even have a video camera."

This is why Status relies on industrial shelter and fencing to protect products purchased on hobby whims, then stored or displayed, preserved for the moment they might be used again.

This becomes expensive, and creates frustrating galleries of personal indecision.

At Baseline, products keep moving.

By the time you have your script together, the camera will have arrived.

Child Abuse

It makes sense that an aging society would begin to place all its chips on youth. But it's an indicator that we'll just be passing the torch, not putting out a flame way past its usefulness.

Hitting any stop button cannot be confused with quickly adding a massive new amount of personal free time for the elders nearing the end. The system stop button must be found, or a bet on youth to jump start a new cycle of nothing more than the same consumption and arguments is child abuse.

Random Acts of Behavior

I'm big on the whole hiding-in-plain-sight principal of suspicion dismissal. San Franciscan's are so nonchalant about public pot smoking that slithering into bushes to lite up a speed pipe simply begs for incrimination. Acting like The Fugitive when you're doing drugs can get you in trouble at Baseline. Same goes for urinating, blow jobs, hiding food, drinking alcohol, or smoking a cigarette. Yes, cigarette smoking is banned in Golden Gate Park. But your dog can shit there if you pick the defecation up. I've taken several dumps in Golden Gate Park, and on a few sidewalks to boot. You never want to poop near potential camp sites, so you back into the bushes and level your behind for projectile shitting, pulling the rear of your pants as far forward and away from your output as possible. There is no place to hide when you poop in the open. Your expression gives you away, or your timing is lucky and you're alone. Hiding-in-plain-site isn't recommended here.

Speaking of speed, many smokers cover their head with a shirt or jackets so police can't testify they saw a piezo pipe in use. The result is a look similar to a hostage being transported or a person getting a hot steam facial. This childish hands-over-the-face hiding makes no sense in a city speckled with Cheech and Chong caricatures and paraphernalia. Unlike pot, get caught by police with a piezo pipe and you have to take the ride. At an identifiable distance a piezo pipe looks like any small glass pot pipe might look in a city of millions of pipes, and smoke looks like smoke. Smoking shamelessly in the open is the safest way to avoid suspicion of speed, as long as you stay distant of visible police. Don't get caught. Exoneration won't arrive before a years of court dates, some waiting in jail, and a whole lot more paranoia on your plate.

This enforcement level will slowly recede as the bench already takes account of the ineffectiveness of intolerance towards speed. Outside law enforcement no one gives a hoot.

The justice system is a cab ride you're forced to take after being accused. A locked cab that speeds past all the places you've ever been, and leaves you stranded with a crippling fare, far, far away from where you once were.

All punishment for non-violent crimes is front-ended now. The jail time after arrest is all you will do, however long they want to keep you which is up to 45 days by police discretion. There, you've been punished before you saw a judge. Everything after that is a few signatures from you and out the door you go. More often than not the case is dropped. Why not? Time was served, length decided by the arresting office's precinct, not a judge.

"You did 30 days for open container? I thought you said they dropped the charges?

Sleeping

I slept in the park when I first entered Baseline, following Harriett who knew every step and could see in the dark. You can't imagine the soulful release that outdoor sex allows until you actually live outdoors. No temporary camping. A committed relationship with the Earth as home and provider prompts out-of-body visibility and extended orgasms that require less physical input, yearning more for the mental input traded in affection and oneness. The aftershock deserves more room than Room 216.

Not sure about sex on the sidewalk. Neither of us ever tried.

We drew too much attention when we slept on concrete. Mostly because Harriett has a Dr. Seuss Mobile. Connected box cars loaded with products and stuff rolled along on bike and lawn mower wheels. Harriett's excess supplies are not inventoried or budgeted. Things are nice to have when there, but you don't think about them if not.

Still, Harriet made it work to move around. The rig, dog, bike, squeaky wheels because she won't ask Scott for some oil, exhausting. I lugged it around out of love, and in the rain when no one seemed to care about it suddenly, and it damn near killed me. Harriet can pull it with two fingers when she wants. Particularly when she's leaving me.

A week-long San Francisco storm moved me back to the sidewalks worried about water and wear on my laptop. Swirling low clouds dripping a non-stop shower that pushed fog to street level and hushed the city into meditative silence. Breakup weather.

Andrea turned me on to a covered garage entrance on Oak that didn't have a No Trespassing sign posted near it. Come morning I'd dry my sleeping bag on a central heating vent on the library floor, right beneath where I sat and worked. I felt like I was catching on to this homeless thing in style while everyone else was soaked, especially the kids.

What Andrea found for me was nice. A small covered garage entrance with a motion activated area light that gave me 5 minutes of reading time. When it went dark I'd just wave the book up for five minutes more free time, and so on. The range of the motion detector extended halfway to the street so pedestrians triggered it walking by. Flash and there I was all sprawled out. This spook house surprise terrified a lot of people when from the dark I'm suddenly seen sitting there only feet away like I'm ready to pounce. A flash then a homeless guy caught in strobe freezyness with his hands in his pants and chewing something while he catches the crumbs in a book. I've since gone back to see this garage and it looks so much smaller.

The later you stay up the less likely the car you sleep

next to will move. Not until the owner has to drive to work in the morning. Watch the street cleaning signs which mark the days the car you sleep next is prone to be moved any time, early, before driver's have coffee, possibly crushing you to death as it departs. If you're not run over, the car's departure has exposing your sleeping location to police driving past. They ticket more on cement than in the park, probably because they think people are watching from their houses.

Note; Make sure you don't sleep behind a planter or a row of vases, or close to anything that a pedestrian might piss on in the dark.

I would always bed down quickly on the street and wake up early. Find a shadowy spot on the sidewalk, drop the gear and pull out the sleeping bag and climb inside before someone gets near enough to see that you're awake. My experience was Status was always more empowered to ask you to move if they saw you awake, than if they had no idea what you were. If I appeared to be asleep I was almost always left alone.

After returning to the park it took me about five months to begin really relishing sleeping late instead of forcing it. That deep to the bone sleep late feeling on bundled warm happiness – a state I found unreachable on the street.

For a while I thought I could always sleep late in the park because if you don't get ticketed by 6am then the park's open. I can remember waking in the bushes on bedding laid out by Harriett wondering beneath sunrise if we needed to pack up and go.

"Nope," she said making a sandwich. "Park's open now so we'd just picnicking."   Albeit our picnic was taking place inside the brush adjacent to the tennis courts where lessons had begun.

Once I slept on scaffolding, second story, tied down with a belt like a mountain climber. Scaffolding is covert and very calming. But you have to be off early because work crews roll in at dawn. Slept right inside an occupied house on night too. The ground floor was being remodeled and was sealed off, but the front entrance was just a door leaned against its foyer. I slid the door away and walked in. A tile hallway leading to an open backdoor I could see the backyard through. The occupants were upstairs, could hear them walk. I set myself up near the rear, smoked some pot and slept. Or thought I did. The specter of being caught trespassing inside was too great to relax. I think I left around 3am, then just walked around.

Sleeping reveals such character at Baseline. Look there and see Andrea, camouflaged in gated gardens, dreaming in a wicker chair waiting to be picked up Sunset Scavenger. Turn and she's fitted creaseless in white sheets on a queen sized mattress, sleeping perfectly sound and at peace like Snow White. Her lovely hands just over the folds of the sheets smack dab in the middle of Page Street, undisturbed. No cars honking, everyone going around. Right in the middle of the street. Looks like a wax sculpture. The wind slows. Haunting is the feel.

Rock Free and I have kicked around a few spectacular ideas for advanced Baseline sleeping and camping systems. Each designed to trick the eyes or freak people out.

We mocked up a prototype of our Standing Sleeping Bag. Made of baton-absorbing polyester, The Standing Sleeping Bag's four legged base supports a parade seat with a seat belt. Once fastened in and standing, you zip the bag up from the inside all the way over the face. The small footprint sleeper defies sit and stay regulation. And with no dress code in San Francisco (you can walk around naked) the Standing Sleeping Bag is a perfect way to confuse police while you confess you've never had a more relaxing slumber, and no one's gonna dare cow tip you. Comes with two disposable adult diapers and sleeping parties of at least three occupied bags is recommended.

The Inflatable Car never made it off the drawing board. But it's just like it sounds. A full color photo-realistic life-size blow up VW Bug or Mazda with a trunk opening to a hollow interior. Use your imagination. Park it as long as there's enough stuff in it to keep it from blowing away, and watch out for street cleaning days, sharp objects, and burning cherries.

Do you Reek?

Last week I spotted a woman who appeared to be the type I could approach without running away. This happens every so often depending on how you behave as a Baseliner and how odd the situation feels in the run-up. For instance, I was sitting in my hillside bungalow one afternoon when a spooky kid wearing a Safeway uniform crept up the hill in front of me to smoke pot or do something in hiding during what I guessed was his break time. He didn't see me until I gave him time to inhale, then shouted out "Nice day to write a poem, yes?" which fell off my tongue a lot flatter and less welcoming than I'd intended it to be.

The kid literally froze, tensed up wearing a distant stare until his glance shot over to where I sat behind the brush. I waited for him to say something but instead he jumped up on both feet, twirling 45 degrees left in the air and upon landing ran away down the hill as fast as he could, genuinely terrified.

The woman I approached last week was different.

"Hey there. How are you?" I asked her. "Let me ask you real quick. You're clearly smart and cool and not freaked out about me speaking to you, so I was wondering."

She smiled.

"Do I smell bad to you?"

Her smile widened.

There was no honest or safe answer for her. I realized

this only after I heard myself ask the question. She could lie about a stench rising from me and say no I smell fine, playing it safe so not to upset the homeless guy. Or she could say yes, I stink and why did I bother asking? Or she could say nothing and send the same message.

I tried to qualify my question. "Sorry to ask you," I said. "It's just that I'm around folks who might not be able to smell me over their own scent. I was looking for a third party opinion so I know if I should get deodorant or something. Me, I can't smell anything."

She took a step forward and inhaled.

My mention of buying something – deodorant – somehow validated the moment for her. She smiled and even nodded approvingly as she said: "No. You smell fine."

I smell like all Baseliners smell who perform simple hygiene when they feel they need to. I smell perfect.

Even my ass smells naturally fine, and I used to flinch from the smell of my ass so much that it became infatuation. Now, it's just my ass. Six months without a shower and no smell at all really. Nor my nuts, or my underarms unless I get high on speed, so I keep a small applicator of Speed Stick which I apply to cover the sour odor that alien drug generates. An organic body at stress free Baseline does not require deodorant. Why would it? Why would a sweat gland rot from stress and anxiety on the body? Run for the Gold and the pressure is on. Run across a field for a friend at Baseline and the pressure if off. You don't smell. Why would an artificial product excuse an artificial activity? Unless it excused a man-made cover-up to, well, cover up the results of an artificial activity? Did the creator of all things leave us to body odor just for kicks to see how long his intelligent flock would take to discover deodorant chemistry? Waiting for us with the big brains to show up and fix it? This logic work for you? You're saying that we're God's superintendent of nature? If so. Where are the keys? Why all the self-doubt? Paint jobs over perfection are con jobs. Cosmetics are not clothes. Go naked.

Remember (Oh, here we go again...): There is no such thing as a man-made necessity. People have never created anything that people really needed. All creations by people only introduced new choices for people to decide upon.

What do Baseliner's really smell like?

If you haven't walked up to one and asked, or recently had sex with one, male and female Baseliners using only water and any type of hand soap found in a public restroom perspire a calming and pleasantly tame natural scent that, unlike the pervasive public broadcast of perfumes and colognes, can only be detected close up. You know, when matters smells most. Baseliner body surface scent is reassuring familiar and consistent for everyone. You stop noticing it unless you really dig in and hunt for it. It's a very quiet odor - does nothing but remind the nose it's still operating. Good example: Smelling a Baseliner is like sniffing through a wool sweater for fresh pound cake that's topped with salt.

Urination, defecation, flatulence, orgasms, sneezes, hair, ear wax and foot fungus all emit this neutral Baseliner scent that keeps kisses fresh, tongues satisfied no matter where they roam, and clothes cleaner between whatever the drummer uses.

Status readers who ignore *The American Homeless Companion*'s urgent call to abandon Status may not see yourselves ever being at home as a Baseliner in Golden Gate Park. You may not even bother to burn some vacation time to come out and try Baseline living yourself. The whole thing is just plain disgusting.

To this readership, we say smash the mirror.

At Baseline your body hits the reset button, and the absence of mirrors at Baseline unbridles your mind to allow positive physical change to take place.

Mirrors and reflective surfaces overwork us on constant

reappraisals of our appearance levels and help us candidly see other people at a level of detail that honors self-absorption. Without them grooming becomes a broader, natural stroke. Tiny plucks and trims and frays and scatters picked up by close inspection are no longer landscaped away, and Baseliners quickly become more naturally beautiful from the reduction of detailing and design, of the primping, loosening and unraveling that interfere with personal look.

The less you organize your look at Baseline, the more organized your look will always appear. This truth works at Baseline the same way the advantage of having only one set of clothes, or some single look at the time: You radiate consistency and stability, and risk becomes unidentifiable following any significant change or cosmetic retrofitting.

Appreciation of the earthy, organic, windblown beauty radiated from the natural grooming habits of Baseline makes it painful to witness the visible decay rates of the cosmetic veils that malfunction on the faces and bodies of Status, who spend money on them for their sales pitch of more.

A diluted fragrance, a chipped false nail, smeared eyeliner, these are each cosmetic refresh cycles which have prospered by avoiding the embrace of usage instructions. Like the Candy Rack we talked about, the shampoo instructions "Wash, Rinse, Repeat" do not provide a choice of when to stop. There are a massive number of choices of types of shampoos and flavors and claims, but there is no choice given on how or when to stop using it.

Which is not as silly a decision as it sounds. Just unfortunately shocking when you are given it. When Los Angeles Fox affiliate channel station WUPW began broadcasting in 1988, then a newbie to the world of the big three networks, the station ran a PSA every half hour or so during the day. A house ad similar to the reminder Nintendo offers Wii Game players to take a break. A 30 second cartoon reminded early Fox television viewers to "take a break, have a walk outside. We'll still be here when you get back."

Unheard of. Look where that experiment went.

The cosmetics industry is awash with bad choices. It's a living bad choice. Take a look at a bathroom cabinet or a sink or shower area. Save the jewelry box and the clothes closet for another essay.

If you still have loved ones speaking to you after you move to Baseline, Hygiene is going to be right up there as the first question that comes from their mouths. "How do you do it? How do you keep clean?"

What was I ever doing blowing seven bucks for a bottle of something that I didn't need to use. Or three bottles of that kind of product that each essentially do the same thing? Is granular detailing of our bodies a worthy pursuit? Is it a fair, or even humane pursuit if its success can only be judged by the creation of a class who fail to conform to a similar level or detailing of the body?

Hygiene is a personal, blended choice. A person who allows anxiety to metastasize into a souring sweat glands may also insist on brushing their teeth each day after lunch. Many Baseliners enjoy wearing makeup. And haircuts can be a fun, harmless expression that grows back. Cosmetic expression is abundant at Baseline, just like smart phones, PCs, and other means of Status expression that are adopted and updated in wide-reaching marketing trends.

Baseliners could give a hoot, but the cosmetics industry takes itself real seriously, and Status is pummeled by its encouragement to take never-ending avenues away from nature. To aspire to looks that resemble artificial life. To define improvement as being less, not more, like yourself.

No Baseliner looks or smells exactly the same. Never the same jewelry, or adornments. The cosmetic copycatting of two teenage girls learning to apply eyeliner at the same time does not exist in Baseline, nor does the process of learning to wear, apply or handle any product related to fashion, an exercise typical in Status that creates almost comically high instances of imitation.

Baseliners do not have bad breath.

They may have beer breath occasionally but halitosis is a Status condition like underarm odor, a symptom of Status related stress and anxiety.

The artificial need for skin lotion falls away at Baseliner since Baseliners typically don't strip away their natural body oils every day in a shower full of detergents. Same goes for eye drops which begin to sting your eyes after a few months at Baseline. No one cares about red eyes.

While we're in the medicine cabinet, Baseliners don't get all worked up about an impending flu season because they aren't alerted by warnings about one. Baseliners don't get the flu the world wants you to trade in. That means no cold medications. No aspirin. All that stuff that builds up while you still feel bad. You do not miss these products, folks. It's as if they were invented solely to have something for people to talk about when they feel ill.

One of the roommates on Potrero Hill forgot he put a frying pan in the oven then set it out to cool. It burned the shit out of him when he gripped it. Worst burn ever. Idea-less, frightened and in pain, he ran off to the store and spent the last of his money on products that advertised they could make being burned feel better. A spray and a cream which neither worked. They were each bad choices in a panic situation. Something for a loved one to buy to demonstrate beyond love that they want to do everything in their power to help.

This from a growth industry like pharmaceuticals that invents brand new diseases that never existed before (we're looking at you, restless leg syndrome) so it can create demand for a drug compound it came up with that has some noticeable reaction to it, along with a trillion other ways to kill you.

Needed or not? To my surprise Band-Aids are not in vogue at Baseline. I thought they would be the rage.

Some Baseliners actually frown at them Band-Aids. The adhesive strips soften the healing surface of the wound making it vastly more prone to re-injury. The proposed value of a Band-Aid is to prevent infection, but the body is way ahead of us here. A little puss (which is an infection) forms a solid scab that blows a Band-Aid away at Baseline. Scabs are tough and don't have an adhesive strip to collects dirt and flake away. Oh, and scabs cost nothing.

The Holy Trinity of Eugenia Grimes

Haste makes Waste.

Sticks and Stone may break my bones but words will never hurt me.

Never feel sorry for yourself.

Sure, but you're my slave.

Labor slave rebellions don't function in the process slave society we adhere to.

All past rebellions enlisted enemies to unite against. There being no real enemies or guilty parties is why they only succeeded at gun point.

The slogan on the Baseline flag could read: "If all the stuff is built what the fuck left is there for us to do?" According to process slavery:

- The plantation owner is the slave. A million dollar a year business can now be run by one person. The sole employee, the slave.
- All value is rated on potential worth, not current value. So youth emerges as industrial captain.
- All enforcement and reward is slave to slave, at all levels. The government is the largest plantation, there is no recognized lower level than slaves. Therefore homelessness is not recognized.
- "Everyone hates their job" is an upwardly mobile fashion statement.
- Slaves have decision making power only over product choices they can afford.
- Slavery is an option, everyone is free to leave. Freedom is never spoken of but all are free to leave.

This means we can all stop working anytime. All of us. Stop what it is we are doing as a job. If you don't have some inspiring muse calling you to get up and go then don't go.

If you want to do something else with your life other than burn away its irreplaceable moments as a business component of someone else's industrial mechanism (which covers most jobs) then escape to Baseline.

Get up now, or sit down, whatever fucking posture that's required for what it is you used to do.
Quit your job.

Get to Baseline.
You won't hurt your Boss. There is no real Boss. Just schedules designed to accommodate business models placed alongside of each other with just enough time to meet and mingle.

That woman over there, know what she does? Her job is billing electronic switching suppliers. That guy next to her is responsible the computer program she uses, designed to keep inventories of tar and steel re-bar from growing too large during an off season.

They don't know one another.

But that guy's company operates solely to support the computers the woman uses to perform her job, which revolves solely around providing maintenance to a single, specific type of equipment that lays down cement roadway. The only cement mixture certified for use by the Federal Highway Commission. The contractor building the highway supports a law that would make it illegal not to have a cement ramp rising to both sides of an elevated public entrance. Estimated cost, $3,500 a pair.

The contractor just hired a part-time temporary employee named Kelsey to complete a direct mail campaign project aimed at passing the new law and works from a list the law firms bought for $7,500. Media advertising will determine a cost-per-thousand viewer advertisement rate used for 15 second messages aimed at injured people who watch The Daily Show. We're just playing with one another. Everything's done, we're only building games now to wrap around mundane tasks also mostly carried out by computer. Say hello to apps. The gamification of all things. Without them, what's the

attraction? Just plain work?
We have not been able to see the fabric beneath the adornment. When did we miss the sign that warned *You Have Passed the Point of Only What's Needed.*

But now, as you tear off your company door key or name badge, ask yourself: Why, at every economic level, no matter what the raise takes you to, or how low the rent is, no matter how tightly you budget your money, you have the same relative amount left over for discretionary spending after every pay check? If you are legitimately earning traceable, upwardly mobile higher income and performing calculated spending restraint that should yield higher savings rates, why are you always the exact same amount of broke?

At the $20,000 a year clerk shift and then the $50,000 a year store manager job.

Eventually as the $80,000 director of product marketing. And always just as broke, falling just as short. Don't bullshit yourself with that "the more you make the more you spend" garbage, which barely qualifies as information, much less wisdom.

Why does the cost of sheltering, supplying and insuring a responsible and fruitful livelihood (not even mentioning a child yet) at any socioeconomic level spanning poverty to upper crust require a minimum 40 hour work week? What's supposed to be taking place with this system we ourselves created? What's supposed to be happening if people only end up with barely enough to get by after contributing all of their worth? At any level.

This is the algorithm at work. Our work.

What we assigned ourselves to accomplish in its plenitude is now waste. We create garbage to keep from laying people off. To prevent from reducing hours. We think we are trapped.

There are not enough things to do anymore at most jobs. So a mountain of stuff is being made and shuffled around for no other reason than keeping people from complaining that their wages are being cut.

Why would we assign human suffering to be one of the measures of result? Would you do that to a person you love? Who said its okay to pretty-up injustices to a person's quality of life if stories of painful, medicated endurance from hours suffering begin to appear?

On the opposite pole, the wealthy elite is too undocumented, restrictive and private to coordinately assume its media-glamorized station actually is as superior to any other level as it likes to appear.

The falseness overflows.

Wealth appears to be nothing more than a fraction adjustment on the currency.

In Status, the minimum ante for most anything that requires the presence of someone who pretends to care is $20. That's what it costs to play unless you are grabbing a product off the shelf to hand to a cashier.

At Baseline the minimum ante is $3.

Three dollars.

If you come rolling into Baseline like you are going to take that $20 target you aimed for and loom it into $100 or more, the Banshee cries for your business model - a model surrounded by $3 antes.

Your big capital disappears in small drips.

This is why new comer kids at Baseline get pissed at Baseline's perceived cheap-skaters. Because these new people bring in with them Status formulas that rely on capital. At homelessness, there is no capital.

Reflections

Enough of this shit, you say to yourself at one point.

The Baseline experience you bragged about has soured. You feel like an outsider again. Back in Status, paranoid and anxious. You experience a moment of clarity. You ask yourself: "Has the gravy train of homeless abundance turned my muscles of due diligence into useless flab, making any future undertaking completely uninteresting to me unless it's dressed in the most phantasmagorical absurdity, like Harriett's ambition with the solar-powered sewing machine."

Your question goes unanswered. All you'll probably know is that you have been so brutally motivated by the dearth of practical and organized behavior at Baseline, that from here on out you'll survive anything. Any tragedy. Any change to the economics of society, great or small. Isn't that so truly American? Wanting to believe in something, then embracing it only to be let down by the little disappointments, the gray underbelly of the whole damn thing?

Proud American, now even homelessness has disappointed you and let you down.

You come out here and its love and peace and you beat the system then your ass hurts and sores from carrying a backpack over a dirty shirt welt and sure you're getting physically stronger but at the expense of many things, that albeit probably unnecessary, do come with their separation anxieties and withdraw symptoms.

No one cares, you remember. Impatience builds.

Stay outside.

A walk through the Mission District. An uninhibited

urban rapture bellowed by a wild-eyed moon-mad Puerto Rican on 16th. He sees the van pull up and shouts “food not bombs” over a neighboring mass.
He then yells “Felice Navidat” across the crowd in glee and anticipation of being fed for free. He dances with a full dinner plate high up in the air with one hand like a waiter on nitrous oxide. Everyone is secretly wishing it would spill to the sidewalk. Dim the lights on the guy. It’s a feeling of sadism and failure pornography which you don’t find as often in the Haight.

The fucking people start to get to you, these utter children calling themselves Witchcraft or Purple, or whatever their road handle de jure is.

The guy says he just biked from San Jose where he was released after three months in jail for “carrying a pipe.” It must have been a speed pipe, but he didn't say.

Why does everything around here revolve around freakin’ drugs?

“Hey, check out the wet pot we found on the freeway. I haven’t even opened up those bags yet. Maybe someone threw all this out in a car chase?”

Chargers with no device. Baggies with empty baggies in them. Lip balm. All junk.

Pot, pot pot. Dope, dope, dope. Who's got the acid? Seen any Molly? Trees and doses. Good black here. Hash oil? Who’s got a green screen? Nuggets? Too many drugs... Can’t, breathe...

We sit in the library and lay all over the damn furniture and fall asleep looking like we’re scrolling through a smart phone that actually has no service and no battery and there’s nothing going on because we’re NOT HIGH YET.

Yeah just wait to get high. And instead of looking normal let your face slack down like a goddamn stoner asshole until everyone looks at you and thinks you are an idiot. Can you try and look any worse? Slump over more, look more wasted, if possible.

You don't want to do anything but get stoned. Your ideas are loony and no wonder you all thought I was a cop.

Rat Bite

Last night, I was bitten by a rat. I didn't see it in time. My right hand. I ran out of money for beer. Upset. I was asking for it. A plastic jar of Planters unsalted peanuts right where my exposed hand hung out of the sleeping bag. I reached down to snuggle in, then from sleep I feel this amazing force on the cuticle of my right ring finger. Venom was my first thought and then some kind of shit needed that was supposed to hurt worse than the bite. It was all clamp. Two punctures, top and bottom, pure force for maybe two seconds. I'm waiting for the punctures to turn blue or black or my mouth to froth up before I go to the Haight Ashbury Free Clinic, otherwise I won't know if I really got anything bad from the critter's saliva in a tad of my blood.

Maybe not having any beer last evening made me a little irritable. I was yelling at a small raccoon I thought was a baby but am beginning to think is suffering from stunted growth. He wouldn't stop trying to break into an older jar of Planter's that was empty of all but aroma. I told him he was a retard and then his pal tiny took a whack to my finger.

I'm changing camps.

Manners

Manners were introduced, glorified and programmed during a period when we were dangerously outgrowing our natural food supply. That said, it makes sense that manners were designed by wealthy people too weak to fight off hungry savages that saw nothing but yummy food for their tummy, so let's think more strategically about manners for a moment.

In 1995 I was one of the relishing drunken guests at a huge barbecue convened around a steel-frame house overlooking Canyon Lake just outside of Austin, Texas. The host who was at ramming speed towards inheriting his father's massively successful steel-frame housing fortune ("Can't blow one down in a tornado, know what I mean?") hadn't put enough fire to the brisket which didn't reach almost-rare until midnight. Guests had been drinking all day, were famished. The side dishes were long ago licked clean. Empty jars of olives, peppers and salsa lined the kitchen. The nearest store was a round trip hour, and by the time guests like me realized the main course was over the convenient stores were preparing to close. These were professionals, thoroughbreds of the Austin software scene and marketers for Dell Computer, et al. By about 2am, when that brisket was close enough not to have a cold interior (there was no microwave at this lake party) guests stood around the brisket and carved it into slices they gagged on as they choked it down. We almost killed the dog sloppily allowing such huge slices to hit the floor.

Here are your manners when the going gets starved, circa 1995.

Manners typically change depending on the food you eat and where you got it. Food is a joke at Baseline. It hemorrhages from every seam. You see the industry of food at Baseline. The attempts to make money. The abundance of your world's food supply shaped through the Play-Doh Fun Factory that architects Status-based consumption. Food has become Universal, so therefore manners no longer are, and good manners should not be an aspiration. They are a side effect. Poor folks don't need to share so much, and rich folks don't have to pretend they have discipline by plating up small, stylish portions.

Everyone eat.

Meet My Neighbors

Why have I had a beef with every next door neighbor I've ever had, even as a child?

I've never made excessive noise, had a loud argument, sent a nasty look, nothing. In fairness, perhaps it was always me who all these past neighbors had a beef with, and my recollections are only the confrontations, not my guilt.

People you really get along with in Status are typically the people you travel some distance to be with, not the people you ask to borrow a cup of sugar from.
The popular observation that has laughed this pitiful reality away since the dawn of the suburbs has been that television and media divide people in groups of shared interest and taste unrestrained by proximity. So why bother with Joe next door when you can spend time with someone very similar to you who you met at the mall, not at the mail box. Nothing is stopping you from choosing far away friends over working it out with Joe just because you'll save gas not having to travel. Everything from exciting pictures of other people and places to the availability of transportation and free time is encouraging you to do so.

The American Homeless Companion disagrees that media devalues the attraction of local community or in any way is the reason you can't remember Joe's last name.

Note: Lots of people in the world like Joe and know a whole lot more about him than you. Don't feel sorry for Joe.
Listen: The dependence on shelter for the preservation and protection of possessions that can be destroyed by exposure to weather or lost to theft became a duplication

industry early on. Demand for sprawling cookie-cutter shelter increased with the population and was less a burden than an investment back into a community. What made home ownership a dream in America was the arrival of easy mobility, the car, not the home. People could move around more easily and get places more quickly. Car-based settlement patterns were designed in, then two forms of shelter sprouted from pure necessity:

- Short term: Pre-built rental structures of all sizes: Hotels, rental rooms, flop houses that could accommodate rapid, mass arrivals of people in a more efficient way than building suburbs (Which was a longer-term investment risk which would require the specter of "homelessness" to keep occupied).
- Long-term: Personalized structures applying developments in art, media, entertainment, fabric and furniture design and landscaping (Private homes).

We settled on these two models, and only then the American Dream of home ownership was hatched. Ownership based on credit, long term investment, the illusion of appraisal, and the accepted but not written law that it was illegal not to occupy and possess for-cost shelter.

It wasn't media that encouraged The American Dream and industrial shelter in tightly knit communities, also known as the mishmash of modern neighbors we have today. Media's own early aspiration to be regarded as a social core killed Media's chances there. Industrial shelter encouraged The American Dream by calling media out as, in fact, a divider.

Fingering media as a divider (not a core) totally disarmed media just when media was ready to keep in a check a country charting into unknown territory after World War II. And once you poison the reputation of a platform like media in a way that questions all of its past and future results it never escapes skepticism. Media, humanity's proven great core, never happened.

Media as social core went to sleep and woke as merely a way to see a lot more without having to travel to it.

Blame always comes to roost with the products we place ahead of ourselves in terms of importance.

How do we stop forcing people to behave in certain ways just because something has been built ahead of time, in anticipation that the forced behavior works as planned? Ala fearing not having a house.

"It's just rich people. We got nothing," is a stupid answer.

Wealth does not describe the descendants of the first people who figured out everything was nothing and made the world what it is today. There was no money until they created it, so by their actions an instincts you would not be able to compare them to the modern day super-rich.

The children of that group on the hill long ago were ordered by their families in so many words to keep their traps shut if they were to remain vested with the generational secret of the genesis of their superiority. They and other offspring families who today only gamble with one another without risk of outsiders polluting the flock or ruining the consortium are a closed group with primitive ancestors who stood upon that hill and looked down at the rest of the folks in their tribe. They understood how commerce was developing and how people more trusting and less intelligent than they were would buy into intangibles like trades and fiat currencies.

This group on the hill did what any of us would do for ourselves and our families, no matter how staunchly we deny it. They realized for the first time that in a commerce society that now made it possible for someone not to farm or hunt, the ones who had the money would not have to work at all.

Purple is the royal color
Long on sacred blood
Twisted genes and noble means
The holy trade in vesslehood

That's it. That's how simple a system it was that they froze and handed down. Don't forget this was still relatively primitive man, so a relatively primitive scheme is what they got away with. Nothing loaded with derivatives or behavior algorithms.

This also suggests that this group's ideals would have to be similarly frozen in time. They would still be products of the primitive conditioning applied to their early ancestral relatives. This primitive, hostile conditioning would have to remain virtually unadvanced for the original back-end of commerce and wealth to remain immune to deconstruction in broad daylight.

This means primitive man still runs the world

If you live on planet Earth, you live on The Planet of the Apes.

Direct descendants of early mankind, bloodlines protected and immune from displacement by war and other incongruity, still walk among us.

I have met one at Baseline Golden Gate Park. His name is Marion Tarlton the Third. He looks like a 25 year old caveman. Exactly what you'd imagine.

He has no details of his family or their whereabouts. He tells me he owns an Edsel, a Tucker, a Studebaker, and a Delorian, each with less than 100 original miles. He's not sure where they are right now. He's a quiet hippy who never wears shoes through the icy morning dew that sparkles Golden Gate Park.

He is a direct descendant of early mankind. He's

skylarking around, or they took his mind and sent him away.

This group likes to fuck around. They aren't dummies, they're bored. They laugh at us making asses of ourselves with it all.

Remember, this group weren't inventors or designers. They were thieves. The descendants of the workers left behind on that hill built this group's houses.

This group can kill people. Who knows how their punishment is dealt. You see a home-made flyer asking for help to find a missing little girl. Her picture is there. The desperate handwriting, her mother's. Why wasn't this missing little girl added to the list of missing children at the end of the 5pm news cast? How many children could be missing who warrant exclusion? What kind of society leaves a mother alone to cry for help to find her child?

This group stole it all. Looted the place and they have had it ever since. These are our mortal slave owners. The slaves are us. They are the answer to why an abundant world offers only imperfect choices, why no one we know is ever really satisfied, not even with decisions about where to live, and who to live next to. Their ancestors meant well. They forgot to put an expiration date on their marching orders.

Where's our paradise, smart phones and all?

We have everything on this Earth to work with and we can't even count on being satisfied with a house we chose from hundreds in a price range we can afford and is supposed to be satisfactory to our station. I mean, there are a lot of economic qualifiers in that last sentence but it just says "Damn, I work as hard as I'll ever be able to and this is all I get? Life sucks."

Why? Why? Why?

Why are a million minor miseries from human growing pains overblown into tragedies that leave scars? The terrible twos, teenage angst, sophomore slumps,

postpartum depression, midlife crisis. And at one point in life don't we all say we hate the place we grew up in, which is why we moved away the first time.
What is always aching at us?

And why all the course corrections when most people can happily say that inside they are the same person they were as a child?

It's because controlling wealth at the top does not give a shit. Or more precisely, they can't give a shit. They are too wealthy to budge, and too far removed to protect people destroyed by any seismic move from the top.
Bill Gates and Warren Buffet may top the Forbes list of world's richest people, but they are far from the richest people in the world. If they were, they could purchase countries. Oust dictators. Backroom stuff. But Gates and Buffet and the rest are only the celebrity rich. Paraded in front of you to make you want to be rich too, and work your butt of for it. One rock star sells a million guitars. One baseball player, a million bats and balls. You see the picture developing. Is it in the best interest of business and industry to build a world where everyone's a winner?

The richest people, the super wealthy whose ancestors stole it all and took charge don't want to be on the cover of Newsweek. They don't want their children kidnapped for ransom. They get all the attention they want. One may be sitting next to you now. Nothing noticeably different. They don't live in floating castles. They like people stuff. They just don't watch a bank balance or pause to think about it. Body guards are for attention go-getter who want to be mobbed. The IRS sees and taxes your salary, but the big loot above is massaged into holdings all over the world that cannot be added up as a single property.

While we have the calculator is out, add up all the names on the Forbes list, then add to that number the gross domestic product of all the countries in the world, then add 10 trillion to that for fun, then another ten trillion for laughs, and you still won't be anywhere near close the sum of all the money that's circulating around the globe as the operational cost of civilization.

That gap between documented wealth and wealth in play is evidence that lots more money is banking on all the things we see around us. Shrink yourself to the size of a Monopoly game house piece and you can feel the familiar anxiety of power above you making decisions that are leaving you with nothing but bad choices.

The super wealthy don't give a shit because they can't. And they are not wining about it. Compassionately moving your house closer to the friend you met at the mall instead of it landing where they placed a blind bet cannot be done when your real game pieces are shipping lanes energy and raw materials. Any move meant to improve individual lives would never trickle down with any accuracy any more than a handful of confetti thrown from the top of the Empire State Building could be promised to land on specific targets. Too many layers of turbulence alters the course on that good deed's journey down through distribution and monetary policy, to infrastructure mandates and local zoning regulations. No wonder there's little distinguishing difference between modern houses. We are lucky to have places to live under this draconian rule. We don't believe this so we apologize with the phrase "It's lonely at the top." That's all we learn about the top.

If a family member of the controlling elite goes rouge from within and starts that crazy talk about changing the world and threatening the family fortune, the source of that problem winds up in a mental institution or is killed.

Keeping in mind this global wealth capture was a disciplined old school decision, would any sensible person not placing short term self-interest over long term family security and indescribable freedom put together a plan any other than this way?

What this wealth controlling group of families share in

common with Baseliners are Earth Right Privileges. Only these two economic levels – at opposite ends of the wealth pole - take advantage of Earth Right Privileges. All those in Status are too concerned with loss to bother with it. Now, this bunch of super-rich. Whose kinfolk stole it all. What are they like today?

Mansions, body guards, secret islands, yawn… Those products are for poor lottery winners exposing how unimaginative their dreams were. However, members of the inner circle are right in front of you every day. The consultant at some nondescript firm thanking the Starbucks cashier. Or the Baseliner handing you a joint.

When you have unlimited spending power it's easy to hide in plain sight. Easy to experiment with being any type of person you want to be.

Earth Right Privileges include freedom to engage in all non-violent activities, free food, and freedom from law enforcement and taxation. You pretty much run the place, you just can't let on. Like Baseliners, the controlling wealth also enjoy the neighbors who live next to them.

The jet setting, tailored, disposable international playground that controlling wealth have at their call should have all the ingredients for satisfaction. And keeping secret this inner-circle lifestyle is smart decision making if you're born to this lot. It's great to have all the stuff you want if that's exactly what you want.

Be your own Boss

Ask yourself this: Could you meet the 40 hour per week financial mark working on your own?

Sure, if you and your spouse want to drool out damp 90 hour work week expressions like "you lose all of your free time" when asked what it's like to be your own boss.

We are pyramid building. Our lives are being taken from us by our own system which neatly rewards owners and management first by enshrining their talent-less contributions on commemorative plaques outside protected public architecture, while the people who wish for nothing more than food, shelter, love and a fair chance to act as they wish struggle alongside the ambitious whose noses are pressed against the glass of self-doubt, never to see the inner-circle. Your position in line is a game of Jacks thrown by vagina's.

"Hey wait a minute! I like my boss, and my job! We've heard this all before! Sure, we're all dissatisfied, but that's life, right? Quit and walkout? How about we'll all get fired! Then what? We begin to starve for nothing wishing we had our jobs back, and if we're lucky enough to get them back we'll be working for less. We'll lose! But that's the way it is because life sucks!"

This is not a drill.

If people, we, are forced to sell our labor and undersell our talent to interests not our own in order to keep from starving, to remain sheltered, and perhaps raise a family, we have no freedom. We are slaves.

Right now, you are not free to do anything but schedule product purchases and product related experiences (oars, yoga mats, bikes, bowling balls) around work.

You cannot pursue your calling, you cannot pursue your personal gift to this world and its people if you are constantly worried about food and shelter. There is no rule saying law abiding citizens have to work, only an unspoken demonic sensation of being held captive not knowing where you are or if it's all worth it. A very strong deterrent against idleness and unemployment called homelessness terrifies people into putting up with even the most demeaning job and slave wage.

Homelessness. You just hear the word. Never a definition of what it means. Just the word homelessness followed by whatever news story gets tagged to the subject.

"A homeless couple was arraigned today on charges of suspected identity theft."

Guilty.

"Crime appears to be increasing as the ranks of the homeless continue to swell."

Guilty.

Let's do this: Imagine our home planet, Earth. The place where you're born, get an education, decide what it is you truly want to do (no matter what people say they need your for) and then hammer away at that ambition with all your remaining days.

"That's an absurd idea. Everyone growing up to do just what they want? It can't happen. Everybody would just want to be a major league baseball pitcher, or a super model, or a rock star."

What is the person above really saying when they shoot down "the absurd idea."

Is the person saying people are not allowed to do what they want on their own planet? Saying people's decision making is the only thing in the Universe that doesn't work properly? Is he suggesting that even though we have more than enough wealth and resources to make everybody in the world a vastly wealthy and happily busy major league baseball pitcher, super model, or rock star that such a thing simply cannot be? Is he just being mean to us? Projecting his own narrow mindedness?

Who says we can't try that world out? Pitchers, models and rock stars all of us, or whatever we decide we want to do.

Of course it would be a mess. So? How have all the other plans we tried to deliver satisfaction to us worked so far?

Certainly, our new pitcher, model, rock star world would encounter a resource and supply challenge fairly quickly as manufacturing reductions of all variety made impact. Remember, not everyone wanted these three dream jobs we just converted the world into. If everyone was on-board - if people were thrilled by the new pitcher, model, rock star world, it could be engineered indefinitely.

However, if we made it to this point of radical reconstruction, something amazingly beautiful would happen.

As "the absurd idea" matured it would certainly change as our current society does. In five years it might be the pitcher, model, rock star, train engineer, baby sitter, farmer, prostitute world, or any number of infinite combinations as people continued to zero in on what makes them most satisfied.

"If you don't get back in there and finish up those orders I'll get someone else who will!? "

The Boss is right. He'll certainly find someone else who will. Someone who likes helping him with his data entry and needs the work for money. Someone who, let's just say, perhaps hated being a soloed mathematician for a pharmaceutical company, or a bookkeeper in Atlantic City, or had no idea why they were in some other job they needed for money they had no passion for so they left, just like the person who originally refused the Boss's orders to get back in there and finish.

When you quit your job, when you walk away from that career which means nothing to your life other than a way to trade your limited mortal hours for bill paying, lots of little messes will quickly arise then just as quickly resolve. Employee displacements, production stoppages, missed deadlines, and canceled orders will erupt and then heal themselves automatically as the migration of people from and to jobs they actually like resets the labor landscape. Remember, the same "hands-off the markets" motto used by Wall Street as a way to convince investors that the markets are always self-correcting works whether or not you are building the economy up, or creatively tearing it down.

All sound too easy? Observe. No government or police intervention needed. People already know what to do. Don't you?

While the Boss conducts interviews for a new data entry specialist, only half of his product orders go out. This startles but has less impact than the words conjure up because the Boss's cost of doing business drops as business drops. Under our new system of walking off the job to pursue your dream job, not as many people will need or want to wear the Boss's catalogue of pizza delivery uniforms, but many still will. The Boss's inventory will go down, he can rent a smaller business office, raise his prices slightly for remaining customers whose customer headcount has certainly increased, and watch margins remain steady at a reduced, more organic sales volume.

This is the re-configuring of the ratios of product types to actual product needs. It requires no science. No enforcement. No instructions. Just mass migration of people to their heart's calling.

Not as much coffee or clothing is needed, local craftsmanship and customization booms, miles driven by automobiles and trucks plummets as less wear and tear on replacement parts of almost all kinds can be counted on. In all, tectonic product consumption requirements will totally reset, arriving at balanced consumption with little waste. Balanced consumption based on people pursuing satisfaction, previously driven by a process slave routine, and just as damn wasteful as we want to be. Ever seen the floor of a painter? The wastepaper basket of writer?

Do we weep for the Boss whose kitchen supply business suffered a lethal drop in sales after 30 years of smooth sailing? Why should we? No one hurt the Boss. His product must have been something a lot of people who were buying it decided they no longer needed.

Besides, other stuff will be needed, and if the Boss likes what he does (which is being a boss, not a bad thing) he'll certainly follow society's lead and follow his own heart and enter a market he likes the most and can handle. That's what Bosses do: Manage a business.

So let's concentrate here, in a new role the boss may want us to call him something different than he was happy being called, like "chef" or "coach." Otherwise no change and a happier guy in a different field. If someone sucks at what they thought they'd be good at, same rules apply. You suck, chef. Are you going to pay someone who sucks at a job any money for doing it? No. And why should you? Because there are only bad choices available? This is why people need to be freed up to plod their own courses. There are thousands of people who know how to build all sorts of cool, interesting, and safe things, but aren't available good choices because they currently work at Frito-Lay. It's only a matter of migration, and knowing one's self.

If you suck, you suck .There are books for people who suck at what they wish they could do.

The end of doing-things-right will not come.

There is no Democratic or Republican way to build a bridge, only a mechanical engineering way to do it.

One thing can be counted on: Following the realignment

of people to jobs, trades and careers, or the nothing they believe they were born to do, industry will not crank out as much product. Staggering trepidation that our new system of commerce will operate or even last - or that promised repayments and reliefs are met – would slow the application of industry to a snail's pace. This would give us plenty of time to use up all the terrible looking shoes we purchase from bad choices run through the shelf stocker.

Listen. Crickets. Note how there is no negative side to slowing industry that you can immediately latch onto other than fewer hours worked.

Prop up everything. Every check. Foreclose on nothing. Clear all debt and print money out the wazoo. Ask for nothing in return. No one loses a dime or sees the value of anything they own reduced or changed from its value in the old system until the whole transition smooths out and the new system of free essentials for living, for all, forever, is firmly in place. How long would that be? Or last?

Last until the old system... the old system... does what? Ask for its money back? Until we call a retired relative and apologize for the fake money system that kept them in terror? No.

We've never pulled out the stops so unconventionally before, ripping away at the simple, the bare, the non-complex layers of the big problems that seemed so resistant to any possible improvement. Never examined the source code of our communication while throwing change management to the wind, never simply given up, accepted loss, agreed to just tear this thing up and start over. Not bulldoze buildings down and start from scratch. What the fuck is the matter with you? Is that where the results of every action you see have to veer off towards? Total failure? Breakage? Why would you or your friends want to break anything? Those people you are defending are your friends? You can do way better than that.

Really. You can live without dreaming about or

romanticizing the need for some bad guy? Who would want to hurt it? Who would want to wreck it? Some evil zillionaire who doesn't want free food and housing for his children's descendants and their friends? It's argued that, sure Mr. Zillionaire doesn't need anything free, he's a zillionaire. This is ridiculous thinking.

"Who is this person?" (Get 'em, boys...)

The freedom and satisfaction illustrated here is what free whole foods and freedom of shelter will deliver to all people. Only dumb imagination doped up on phony entertainment violence interrupts this progress.

Who is going to get in the way of our new system? If something is declared free of charge how can a mafia justify spending money to put the clamps down and make people pay? Pay for what? What is the value? The crime gang also now enjoys free whole food and shelter for themselves and their family indefinitely.

You think some national emergency, some swept forward executive order – or any order - to revert back to the previous paid system is going to fly once you get the taste of free whole foods and freedom to shelter? Nope, not giving that back. You guys just proved it could be free.

What's next then, Debbie Downer? The military sent in to shoot us all if we don't obey and revert back from progress? Really? The all-volunteer military whose soldiers enlisted because they could barely afford food and shelter, and who've just been told food and shelter is free for the rest of their lives and for their families as well..? They're going to side with the old school? And that's if they haven't deserted. Whose next, kill joy? Blackwater mercenaries who take home a Colonel's pay grade for a Sergeant's responsibilities declaring a free fire zone in a Kroger's parking lot? Soldiers won't fire on unarmed civilians in America. That act is way, way past. Isn't gonna happen. AWOL all day long, but lots of people dream of being soldiers and sailors. If lots of soldiers abandoned their posts, aspiring soldiers will be there to pick up the dropped swords. Does this mean Drill Sergeants won't be tough, and the military weak? Would you be feeling weak after jumping into uniform following years of aspiring to be a legitimate soldier?

Besides, a potentially weakened military means only one thing, disaster movie buffs: Russia must invade US soil. Russia watches CNN, Putin perceives weakness in our new system of free whole foods and shelter and decides to invade U.S. soil. What kind of country will Russia be seizing as they witness Americans seemingly going off their rockers?

So What?! is what will happen. We'll all be eating dinner and watching Deal or No Deal when the ruskies parachute in and hit our beaches while some of us stand around and watch and offer the soldiers ways to charge their smart phones and get services so they don't have to tell their loved ones how bored they are in America.

Of course, they drop the A-Bomb. The whole world invades us? There's mass chaos, looting, pillage, famine, floods, locust, a giant earthquake! The planet Earth explodes like the Death Star? Over free whole foods and shelter?

Why would anyone waste their time like that?

None of this will happen. It's all sick, dramatic fantasy we fluff TV shows, movies, books, music, bragging, folklore, lies, lies, lies...

It is already too late to say we have not begun acting at times as if we have actively crossed bridges of the experience that we only experienced through entertainment. Watching TV and thinking we learned it. Kung Fu, hot wiring, organized crime, survival.

Given the flexibility of digital media and an audience appetite for adult content, the most intriguing entertainment would be not reality, but fiction. Stuff we make up because we can now put it on a screen. Stuff that doesn't really happen, cannot happen, should not happen. Murder, zombies, hacking's, fear.

A memory of a movie can now serve just as completely as a memory of a live event. The black and white blend to gray if you are not paying attention, if you are just passively consuming. Don't let "passive" fool you. Passive consumption is your cousin Jimmy jumping to his feet and screaming bloody murder because the Hero 5 Storm Deathonsons game he's lost in on the PlayStation 14 just got its power cord ripped out of the wall because he wasn't listening to a fucking thing any living thing around him was doing. Jumping up fists clenched in a "passive" aggressive rage.

Suddenly we might get a feeling we are in a more dangerous world then we thought. Feel like we paid the dues for actions we never used, required, or really even wanted all that much. Look, the problem with every modern fear from poorly lit streets to escalated doomsday arguments that encourage us to imagine scary stuff like Russians dropping thermonuclear bombs or Lex Luther-style Crime Syndicates forming from freed prison populations, or any other balderdash that some stupid fuck thinks up, is that we forget that our own human laziness and predisposition towards disappointment will result in all of us mostly not giving a damn. We're too lazy for the horrors we dream up. In reality, America could not run up a body count if it tried. Not at home at least.

Just look abroad. On any given day 1,200 Pacific islanders become fish food with one wavy flip of a rotting ferry crossing the Banda Sea. A horrifically tragic event, but very little discussion is spent thinking about a memorial for those lost. The next day a commuter bus in Mexico plummets down the side of a mountain carrying with it 98 doomed and screaming passengers after only doing 45 miles per hour round a corner.

The best we can do is 3,000 or so people during an

event that clearly should have claimed three times that amount. The largest skyscrapers in Manhattan collapse just after weekday rush hour?

Oh, well. It's always the same here in the States. Not as scary as deadly as we were told to imagine. No bloodbaths, riots, or real change that measures up to the magnitude of the event run-up. Just the troop presence and lackluster routines expected in times of national emergency. Never do our initial fears sneak up on us by surprise. Take Hurricane Katrina and the guy charged with shipping back 750,000 unused body bags. What happened to the million dead in NoLo? Only 168 Americans killed in a federal building that housed a daycare center? What? Just two people dead in a Greyhound Bus collision in Santa Maria, California?

Practically everything we are told to fear in American is overblown in its threat. We have a safe, mature society and most people are a heck of a lot smarter than you think. People pick the best choices mostly. The ones that feel safe and well thought out, and from the heart.

Here's a good choice many would consider a bad one, but when chosen becomes not just a good decision, but a good choice that simply didn't read like one in our expect-the-worst world.

The guy who camps nearest me is a murderer who killed a cop when he was twelve years old. Judicial conviction ruined the promise of his life. Drowned out by the murder of a badge is the fact that the dead cop was the guy's father who he caught raping his little sister. The murder weapon was a police revolver. A heroic child in shock and does the right thing at the only moment it would be justified, and 40 years later is released from San Quentin. He believes a choice should be offered to this country to release all inmates from every prison.

By his math, release all prisoners and 80 percent of them would go peacefully searching for family members, loved ones, and children. About 15 percent would be killed by mercenaries paid by relatives of victims unhappy with verdicts and appeased with only settlements. The remaining 5 percent would indeed commit crimes. The victims of these crimes: Other trouble makers. Two hicks in a Greenville gas station get their heads blown off after mumbling nigger jokes. A family of three held in a standoff between police and a released prisoner trying to communicate with his estranged wife who'll soon need treatment for a gunshot wound. Are these few, isolated incidents important enough to prevent millions of children from reunited with their freed parents, some of whom they have never met before?

Is the loss of a few, even hundreds of, trouble-makers too much collateral damage for us to bear during a period of significant, positive change in this country? The U.S. can slaughter 200,000 civilians overseas and call it necessary for the improvement of the culture and the betterment of their people. But no. We can't stomach a few dozen in our steps towards social improvement.

Population-wide improvements to our lives and freedoms are halted in America by just two people, a couple standing on their lawn in Tampa crying to CNN camera's that "this whole thing is simply going to destroy our lives. We simply can't have this in America."

CNN news should be given a journalistic award for being the only news gathering agency to find the only two people in American who don't want whatever mass improvement is on the table for passage.

Cheating in Class – Status Sticks It Out

How should one behave at Baseline after Status is stripped away?

At the end of my junior year in high school I wanted to help a friend cheat a final exam. The faculty had labeled my cheating friend a subpar student, so his answers would not have to be perfect. But I wanted to show off how I knew practically all the correct answers to our English Literature exam, so I fed my multiple choice selections to the guy using numerical finger signals he could count from where he sat in class behind me. The multiple choice answers would all be correct, then he'd take an appropriate markdown in grade by his weak performance on the written section of the exam.

I forgot to pay attention to what I was doing.

As I blazed away the answer codes using my lowered left hand, I suddenly got the sense that the saloon piano had abruptly stopped playing because someone very dangerous had just walked through the swinging double doors.

I looked behind me and my friend was shaking his head, ready to laugh. Our teacher had been standing right there behind me. Saw everything. For how long? I didn't ask. My classmates stared at me in disbelief. The teacher was furiously disappointed. I had been the pupil she trusted to teach the rest of the class her curriculum on those occasions she needed a break.

The test was still in progress, there was half an hour left in class. The teacher drew a dramatically large letter F on my answer sheet. My friend crumpled up his answer sheet.

I was humiliated. But not my cheating classmate. He gallantly asked to be dismissed so he could begin studying for the next period.

The teacher was not going to keep him, but I remained silent and didn't budge. I straightened my answer sheet with the big F drawn on it and began completing the exam. I'd made it to the written essay portion of the test before my plan was foiled, a section of the test my friend knew he'd have to complete on his own. Busted or not, I'd done my job. But I kept on working.

The teacher asked me what I was doing, though see knew.

I told her I wanted to stay and complete the test and hand it in for her review even if I'd just been failed for cheating. I felt obligated to demonstrate I knew what was right after falling from grace in front of my teacher and classmates.

Recalling this moment, I should have followed my fellow failed friend out the door. High expectations for my behavior during the test were shattered. I'd failed the final which was weighted at 25 percent of the class year which meant I'd likely get a D for my A-grade semester. Why was I still there in class? Working harder than I had to, for nothing? Basking in humiliation.

With this incident in mind - a cheating violation on my permanent record that cost me a National Honor Society membership I had to strike from college applications – let's consider how a Baseliner, a person who in the eyes of Status has failed the test of society, is supposed to act in society after being told there's no more use in trying?

When my friend got up and left the classroom after being shown that the Status of his English Literature final exam was zero, Baseline, nothing, I sensed envy from the rest of the classroom.

Without that good choice from the teacher, getting up and just leaving would have been criminalizing... you know, if he just got up and left, or even worse if he just sat there distracting everyone – a cruel punishment for all.

If you believe there are indeed bad people, this shows how bad people are non-disruptive when given good choices, like leave to study, of all fucking things, another final exam. There was never a choice offered to leave the exam. That was not an option for passing. Adding a good choice, or choices, is the right of everyone, and it's never too late to introduce one.

It was me who just kept screwing things up by sitting

there squirming over a final exam I only partially attending to. My embarrassed charade only served to distance the teacher and my classmates from me further, and my academic efforts which once appeared studied now called for inspection of concealed lies. English hero to cheater zero in 32 minutes flat, Eastern Standard Time.

Why did I make the class and teacher have to endure the loss of my cheating as long as I made them to? Because I could be seen. I hadn't left. Visibility drew inspection, which created action.

This is why Barbie and Ken and all their friends never stop smiling. Their Barbie and Ken Dream House, Ranch House, Beach House, Fun house, are all open air. If they had privacy they would drop their veneer, and upon seeing them your little sister would ask "what's wrong with Ken?"

When you catch a glimpse of a Baseliner slowly trudging along the sidewalk in the early morning with eyes half-mast, yawning against the morning sunlight, you wince at the sight of "the sloppy, disgusting homeless." But you see this same sight, same expression and gait, every morning in your hallway. Between your bedroom and the restroom of your apartment. This expression is your wife's, your husband's your grandmother's, your roommates.

That is what you're looking at. Not a mumbling, confused bum slumping from a drug and alcohol hangover. A normal person like your mom who just woke from a night's sleep. Baseliners wear the same expressions your loved ones and roommates wear when the loved ones and roommates assume no one is looking at them: Lumbering motion, bone tired exhaustion, visible confusion, lengthy contemplative blank stares, and shameless unpreparedness. All natural expressions made by people busy living indoors.

Upon this obvious truth *The American Homeless Companion* must question: What is wrong with being witnessed living outdoors?

Are we only allowed to be seen "living" by those who share a home with us? Can't we act alive in all its dramatic range while operating outdoors, and visible.

Baseliners act just like your dad or your brother does during their first stroll to the restroom after getting out of bed. Only the Baseliner's stroll to the restroom is seven city blocks, not yards of indoor carpeting. Your Dad and a Baseliner each drag their feet and appear half asleep after they wake. They each yawn, scratch parts of their body unconcerned by how they might appear. They each nibble on something left out overnight with half the wrapper still on. They each may drink and smoke. In other words they both act identically.

Cops, yeah. Cops.

For over 50 years across the face of this planet I have seen countless thousands of police actions of every manner.

Real police actions. The job, not a person eating a doughnut in the cold, or adorned in dress uniform weeping for a beloved lost comrade. We're talking police actions that that take place in the line of duty.

During all these thousands of displays of police presence and action, I have never seen one thing I would describe as being good.

Not to say it was all bad. It didn't change anyone, for the most part. There was just nothing good, of its own. Even if the cop was just standing at an event like a circus, doing nothing but policing, and in the best mood, chatting with people and laughing with co-workers, the net result of the cop's presence was not good. It was not a good scene.

Period.

An underground railroad

How dare Reverend Ryan of Christ's Church in San

Francisco distance himself from the fact he does good work giving homeless people, Baseliners like Dean and Harriett, access to his church, keys to the doors so they go enter at night if they need, to charge a phone, heat up a meal, watch a porn DVD or *Raiders of the Lost Ark.* How dare Reverend Ryan run from the fact his church buys $200 bike buggies for known drug dealers who are Baseliners. Where is Reverend Ryan's voice in saying to the people of San Francisco "Look, I have opened the church to the homeless, and we have lost nothing. Nothing has been stolen. We have helped homeless fathers replace bike gear they needed to make a living and stay honest parents who pay child support."

Instead, Reverend Ryan flees the facts, making Dean and Harriett look and feel like criminals worried that word might get out they idled about the church nocturnally. Word that they were simply taking Reverend Ryan up on his offer.

If you run into the street and get hit by a car because you're fleeing in terror from a Baseliner, chalk it up to Karma.

The American Homeless Companion condemns those who feel they need to understand, sympathize, give money to, feed, support, or analyze, or use as a political backdrop Baseliners, but only in a closeted fashion. Are we really running underground railroads for today's second class citizens? Helping the homeless on the low down? Fear or cross infection? Doesn't this all sound darkly familiar? How did it all turn out for everyone last time? In the 60s? Resistance to Baseline acceptance is futile. There won't even be any surprises this time around.

Make noise, people.

The American Homeless Companion asks you to become one.

Join us at Baseline.

This is a green-field civil rights movement waiting for

action. Actions creates change, nothing else.

Possessions or people? What is more important? Baseliners I watched leave to Status left because someone in Status loved them. Those who left Status through support programs, low-cost housing, bus rides or government aid each returned to Baseline. Some after a few months, some after almost a year.

"What happened?"

"Very kind social workers. Piles and piles of guilt".

That Gift

Status conversations are boring.

Most of them are social calibration quizzes that test a group's synchronization to a TV show they should all be interested in (say, last night's HBO Season Finale) in order to sniff out who in the group is going astray ("Beth and Herb aren't watching TV together anymore..." "He doesn't watch that? What does he do on a Thursday night?").

Tired of this?

All worn out from supporting the other side of a conversation about Tour de France doping policies and whoever that washed up American star you're familiar with is? You know, the guy who banged Sheryl Crow?

Looking for some real conversation action? Tell a Baseliner you're not a cop and kick up a conversation with them. The cop part was comic relief, but you will need to get that out of the way if you are a white or Hispanic male. Asians are too honest and blacks won't cross a brother with undercover work.

Baseliners won't attack. Relax. Drop formality. Your boss is who you should fear.

Feel the need to test if you're demeanor is telegraphing your tepidness? Say "hi" to the Baseliner's dog first. Fido will tell you how master is going to feel about you deep inside.

The American Homeless Companion recommends this formula for starting a conversation with a Baseliner: Fire off an undisputed truth in mid-sentence such as "No matter how pretty they make it look, ya know?"

This appears to be broken English but notice how its lean colloquialism allows any massively applicable thought to come right on through even if their reply to you is "what?"

Your name is a great conversation opener with Baseliners. Really, just your name.

"Jane."

"Bob. Nice to meet you."

Now hold out your hand if you are close enough for a fist bump. You have Purell in your purse. Proceed to say anything you want, but bear in mind. Baseliners know what's on HBO, but comparing details of last night's season finally best be left at the office. Want to talk media with a Baseliner? Say something true.

"I just have to say this guys, I don't know if you watch TV but more shit comes out of that thing than my asshole."

You're on your way.

Great discourse can be found at Baseline, and why wouldn't it be? Baseliners are Americans born and raised with all the bullshit filling.

In fact, Baseliners can carry on several different conversations at the same time. Overlapping conversations are commonplace in Baseline and they sometimes have no end breaks, they just continue until a Baseliner you are talking to as you walk by falls out of earshot. When you see this person next the conversation picks right up where it became inaudible, without pretense. In Status the sense that powers this interrupted but unified conversation thread style is in use when Status friends rejoin and say "Wow I was just thinking about you." If instead these two friends in Status rejoined with "... hey so that's why those socks we hang are disappearing too, makes sense" they'd be sounding like Baseliners. The friend hearing this sock news would, by the rules of Status privacy, flinch to think people have been talking about him behind their back. He remembers the subject, but in the time since then the treading of Status society overwrote the conversation. Introducing the detail alone appears like others carried the conversation on elsewhere. Classic defensiveness: The sticky stuff of Status that's hard to clean off.

Remember this though: Not all Baseliner's – particularly the old timers – have the best conversation skills. In many cases it's what got them flung from their Status roost, not being able to articulate that the bill was going to be late again in a manner that's very convincing. Maybe they get nervous when they talk and it was okay until they turned 25 and support and patience for that kind of thing was no longer to be found. Like the crooks who won't stop being crooks and the dopers with the big embrace, Baseline has lots of models that Status has never been famous for tolerating. That's why they inhabited Baseline first, the lucky bunch. Nowhere else to go. And didn't want to go anywhere.

Bring your Status conversation to Baseline and you'll find the dirty clothes and the "to hell with it" gait. But you'll also discover, as others walk past and say "Hi" to the bum you're talking to, lots of Baseliners look like they just ended their shift at the Men's Wearhouse or The Gap. Their hair is fly and their clothes are dope and many in Status would be shocked and deeply changed if people they met each day who they thought were Status, were actually Baseliners.

A Baseliner like Lumpy, who you'll read more about later, who wears freshly cleaned, casual clothes – shorts and a Giant's Team Jacket – unscuffed Basketball shoes and pays for his food with stamps. Probably sits right next to you each day during your lunch hour.

Lumpy

His speech. Subject after subject, a word or a phrase with no sentence structure. It takes about five subjects heard against the context of the conversation before you realize he's making sense.

It's like reading Finnegan's Wake. Or a private detective who knows it all and what not to tell you. Dropping case files one by one on a table in front of you. Reciting the names of each involved as the manila folders hit the varnish.

"In a stage. What have you given me. All about time. Places. Rochelle Welsh. Right. Ha, Ha, Ha." Lumpy bangs out of time on small untuned set of bongos.

Listen in on Lumpy during lunch time and you hear him decode his native language so you can understand him. Lumpy watches you eat a pickle, says: "They should ask you if you want those are not, right?"

You crunch in.

"That way they could give them only to the people who really want them."

He's got your attention. Appears to be a little league coach. You talk to him, shoot the shit, laugh, then go back to the office never suspecting the dude you ate lunch with and traded Gmail and Facebook with was a homeless person who sleeps in the park next to the Safeway your family shops in. And that's when Lumpy isn't catching some rest in a cement pipe that workers are digging a hole for on Stanyan Street.

You ate the pickle he really didn't want.

More tips for bridging conversation and striking accord between Baseline and Status.

In front of Baseliners, when making a personal

statement or observation of yourself, its good form to add the higher truth to any formative truth, if in fact one exists.

Confusing?

This would be the formula: So in order to remember to wash my underwear tomorrow, I decided to take them off after I get into my sleeping bag, otherwise I'll go through the motions of dressing and won't want to do laundry for another day. Oh, and it will be easier to jack off too!

Adding an additional layer of The Real helps remind that the thing to do is not always the most important or fun thing to do.

Ignoring Baseliners always backfires. There is no elegant or safe retreat from a conversational opening at Baseline.

Baseliners say hi to everyone they know, at any distance. Especially if the recognized party does not know they have been spotted. In Status, this is an option. In Status you can ignore one another. Not good.

In shopping malls, parking lots, grocery stores, Status has a terrible track record of not yelling "Hi there" when they see a friend or acquaintance. The exclusively Status borne sentence "Hey I saw you the other day at the mall" suggests you were spying on someone. Maybe, but you certainly didn't want to talk to them or for them to know you were there. Status can even rationalize allowing incorrect directions or phones numbers to proceed forward in hopes of throttling back relationships and potential visitors.

Status is a proving ground for being wary of one another, as if we're all ready to attack. Every extension of an arm is going to ball into a fist. Every change in course as you walk is positioning to get close enough to spit, mug, rape, or kill you.

Somebody give me a hit of pepper spray.

Baseliners don't give a hoot about the smart phone you obviously, ridiculously, stash in your purse when you spot a Baseliner passing by – that's Status code for "coming towards you". The thieves that you in Status should be cautious of are your son's friends who know the contents of your jewelry box.

Baseliners who stop and wait on a path some distance ahead of a Status person are not foolish enough to ignore the fact that Status now sees a homeless man with nothing to lose waiting to attack after spotting his prey. The Baseliner may be tired. Watching something else. Who cares? If some 50 years old man on a waiting list for knee surgery stopped on a path ahead of you to rest the same way, you'd probably start thinking up something nice to say. Maybe ask if the man needs help. (See: Picnic essay)

We should each demand with absolute fury why we accept by any measure pure bullshit to this one question posed many ways: "What's it all for?"

Versions of this include "What's it all worth?" "Life sucks and then you die" and an outcropping of colloquial versions which in some cases seem to trigger an effect opposite of what was intended, like "You can't take it with you when you go."

"What's it all for, gator?"
"No one knows, sonny boy."

Whoa, whoa, whoa, wait a minute. What do you mean no one knows?

That's what we're saying with this shuck and jive, right? All this "that's the way it goes" "isn't ours to know" "first your money than your clothes" "if the Lord has willing and the creek don't rise" bullshit.

A why would we be told to wait for this information? Why don't we just call it? After all we're the ones who have lived it here. Surely we can think of some optimistic reason to garnish our cluelessness. Who are we waiting for in order to accept responsibility for our own actions as a culture? Where's the chorus of those who today understand that any debt hung around us is debt we merely owe to ourselves. Who are we waiting for? Jesus Christ? He was already here. What's he going to say we don't already know?

That we, you, me, think for even one second we do not buy into and believe our own answers to what it all means

is wrong. Just ask God. We believe our own gospels. But we need serious reporting from the field, or beyond.
What American needs. What the world needs, is a walking, talking dead guy.

Well he or she doesn't have to be ambulatory, and maybe it shouldn't be a she. Too much of a sympathy risk, some poor woman walking around with flesh peeling off her. Microphones dangling all around her and a sea of smart phone video recorders trained on her around the clock.

So much could be settled if dead person would come back to life. Note, we did not say "could." Some mute promise of light calling us after our vitals tank will simply not cut it here. We demand a highly articulate dead person with a whopper, expert memory.

Jesus, in the Kings James Version, handled three of these thrilling interviews. The Son of God supposedly reeled back into life a widow's son at Nain (Luke 7:11-17), kept the conversation with Jairus' daughter after she croaked (Matthew 9:18-26; Mark 5:21-43; Luke 8:40-56), and how can a movie buff even begin to picture Christ's resurrection of Lazarus without thinking about holding their nose (John 11:1-44)?

Anything uttered by the Jesus Gang of Three won very little copy in the Bible, when you would the think the words spoken by these thee corpses would be in purple or day glow versus Jesus' red in babble. This is lazy reporting by the Israelite s, who had executive editor roles in the named books. Where was the documentation of these priceless people? You'd think what came out of their mouth other than gurgling or bugs would be pedistooled and worshiped.

Well, everyone. These three dead people had very little to say in a world loaded with a million questions for them. Where again, *The American Homeless Companion* demands, where was the reporting of the disciples here? I would have had chisel and tablet in hand screaming for an exclusive. What a game changer too if we'd been witness to three dead people at the same time. All at once, hogging the camera. Each with a totally different idea of life after death.

A few relatively complete sentences from these three or a McLaughlin Group style moment of debate and Jesus would have seen his lines in the bible cut to a supporting role. The more dead guys keep coming on the closer Jesus comes to being nothing more than a cameo.

There had to be at least one really articulate speaker with a fair short term memory who found themselves killed in the vicinity and range of Jesus. Had Jesus bothered to resurrect this guy we'd all be reading his book instead of the Bible. Way more meaningful subject matter, way thicker gruel. Jesus who? Shut up and let the dead guy talk.

This impact has never been lost, or weakened. It waits, compressed to release upon the arrival of the first talking dead guy. At this point in time we might not even declare this person technically back-to-life, or want to muddle things up with religion by calling it a resurrection. Just leave him dead and get on with it. In these modern times it would greatly depend on how long the dead person has been dead. Otherwise the abortion opponents would jump on it. You know, the folks who brought you "hey let's try this case as a double murder because she was pregnant and that way the fetus that was killed would have to be.... Yeah, yeah, all together now.... A human being."

If the dead person really cut the mustard - or it began seeping from his eye – and we're talking dead for some time here, long enough to begin rotting, not minutes, days dead, then we'd be onto something.

"Spiritual one, but what about sin? A lake of fire. Eternal damnation?"

"Come on people, that tale won't buy you a hot cup of

olive oil. It's eternity. Get that? What's eternity? A long time. You can get used to anything given eternity."

That would probably be it for the Bible, altogether. Particularly if the dead guy had some dirt on Jesus. How Jesus really didn't give a good goddamn about returning to save who?

"What is that, spiritual one?"

"Forget it. I don't want to resurrect that whole disaster. I'll just say it's always the family. Always the family."

Mind

From my Mom's side I was born just three generations out of a Southern Baptist family of twelve. In a photo they and other relatives have gathered together in front of what would be called a wooden shack. One with a dirt front lawn.

On the far left is my mother, a child in the picture with the same thoughtful eyes. No shoes.

It's joyous photo. Above Mom is Gammie, laughing, looking exactly like she always did. Perfect in size for her timeless garb and hairdo. Eerily permanent across time at every age I've ever seen her.

One Christmas Eve at Gammie's house in Florida the electricity blacked out at about nine. Lights on the Christmas Tree went as did the room and hall lights. Outside the neighborhood disappeared. Music and TV inside went dead. Mom spoke first reminding us all not to open the refrigerator so the cold would stay in. My Step-Dad, Uncle Lu and his wife and kids from California, my sisters, we were all there, but no one else spoke. No one else moved, even though moonlight filled the room.

Seamlessly into the blackout Gammie kept on playing on the living room floor with my 5-year old niece, Lena. It was easier now to hear the song they were singing as they clapped hands together. Sure they knew a blackout had taken place. That was cool. Neato, no more power. It mattered not.

No one else moved. Anticipating the power returning any moment was good enough.

It was Christmas Eve.

What made Gammie and Lena happy was not tethered to electricity. Here was a woman who'd lived without it during times it was far less reliable, and a child in her final episodes of freedom from a lifetime of electronic distractions. I couldn't take my eyes off how beautiful it was watching the two of them sing their little Christmas song together on the floor.

How many other families in Gammie's neighborhood had their holiday spirit momentarily put on hold while power was restored that Christmas Eve? Families who'd saved all year and traveled to be together. Pictures and moments taking place that will cover and replace so much hurt down the line.

Then, where's the power?

A sense of self-blame creeps in. No one can fix it and there hasn't been a blackout in years so why's it have to be now?

Why us?

It's a hurtful game of gotcha to develop for decade's dependent wrappers around holidays celebrated to emphasize a pure meaning. The dependence on man-made products is the least fair of all. In these moments our spirit does not go dark with the electricity.

Lasting Value

At the apex of my Status I was awarded a set of business cards that read Director of Marketing, United Business Media's Channel Group, because it looked better on a business card than middle-age alcoholic (Thank you, P.J.)

It was a strange ladder climb but a lucky one that made

sense. Stiff-lipped sales needed a loose-lipped artist to script pitches for technology advertising, so up from editorial I ascended.

Poof! Here's your executive title, Mr. College Dropout.

I resigned from the job because I was getting signals that I was about to be fired after I wrote a blog entry for Paige Coverage, a fictitious blogger I created to sell Xerox copiers. The blog was a purposeful shock and awe attack on one of Xerox's biggest re-sellers. I had been told to stir up a little controversy but let fly with no quarter because that same afternoon my wife at the time changed her Facebook interested-in Status from men to women, as if I wasn't going to get an automatic notification so I could begin jerking off that instant.

I was a fast worker. No one in operations of the $3 billion company really gave a shit about anything I labored over so I created weapon's grade marketing material that got in, got out. Take it to your customer motherfucker. Tell your customer what to do which is buy our fucking products and ABC or you get the steak knives. Sales soared under my three year watch. Art on the walls of the executive floor in Manhasset, New York, was being replaced by framed sales contracts I'd have my assistant create after they cleared legal and accounts payable. I always yelled at her that it was million, with an "m", not billion with a "b". We sent back a lot of engravings until she got that shit right.

An executive VP named Dan Dignam actually ran the company while the CEO – a convert from editorial like I was named Bob Faletra - drank with client brass, disappeared for six months for knee orthoscopic, or dashed off emails about business visits to India.

I've never forgotten the impact of a call I got from Dignam after I presented a marketing project that explained to sales how online advertisements could be sold alongside print ads. It was a revolutionary idea to sales in 2008.

Dignam was always screaming in a hoarse manner even if he patted you on the back and said "you're doing good things."

"You know, Dan. Being the fastest. Being the first person to get something done. That's the tactical. Versus the strategic. The tactical doesn't necessarily have lasting value. It's great to be fast, don't get me wrong. It just doesn't have, you know, the same value as strategic thinking. Like DeMarzo, or Toni (both aging execs unable to keep up with younger employees) who look at the strategic."

I know what Dignam was doing. He was trying to give me a break, thinking I was going to age up too with the classic crew, and that I could drop it down a gear.

He was again offering me my career. The lasting value was to my career. Slow down Mr. Director of Marketing and save yourself a few things to do to keep busy so the kids don't see you dozing off. You have a longer way to go than you think.

It hit me. Those business cards with the snazzy corporate directorship title meant I didn't have to complete anything. I just had to try. Completion would be an ending. The loss of a task. I could not accept loss. That was part of my job description.

It was effort, not results that was sought.

Businesses and governments rate themselves based on their input to a problem, not their output, or number of successes. This eloquent observation arrives from P.J. O'Rourke in his 1991 book Parliament of Whores. Every system that fails to deliver meaningful results other than its own self-preservation falls back on this measure of itself. There can never be too little crime, so let's parade all the great police efforts. Never too little poverty but no greater effort has been made than by this administration, and so on... The input measured, not the output.

Why is civilization stalled? Progress towards satisfaction on pause? Simple: All the institutions trusted with wealth far greater than any citizen or opposition keep getting another chance to deliver poor results wrapped in the child's excuse "I tried my hardest."

Let this sink in.

The criminally un-used and neglected power to make people's lives immediately better constantly fails, if it bothers to show up at all. Then always, as if we are fucking stupid, the criminally un-used and neglected power to make people's lives immediately better gets off easy in the face of historic underachievement. In our misery we manage to smile and award it an "A" for effort.

People counting coins from their car ashtray to pay an approaching toll on the way to work are fired if they fail to produce expected results. We accept this as a rule of work.

At the same time reachable satisfaction scuttled by government incompetence.

What the hell is going on?

I have always had a hunch that people at lower Status protect the unequal privileges of those at the highest level of Status because they are convinced they will achieve that highest level eventually, and will want those privileged in tack when they arrive – not missing them because they appeared unjust on the way to the top.

This is how Republicans get construction workers to vote against their own best interest when the GOP gives tax cuts to deep pockets. Go easy on what will all be yours too someday.

Every child in America is told the opportunity to go all the way to the top is there for them. It doesn't exist without promotion opportunity. Even the most obvious dead end jobs promise raises.

"Poverty sucks" reads the poster of Keith Moon, the tuxedo clad millionaire drummer of The Who leaning against a Bentley with top hat and cane smiling down at you shortly before drinking himself to death at a terribly young age.

Your desire to have the things you want when you want them, is not bad at all. Who wouldn't? Smart call.

The American Homeless Companion supports all human ambitions, including the creation of, and ruthlessly blowing of mass piles of wealth. Nothing wrong with it at all.

It appears that social progress towards satisfaction is being slowed by people who don't want change to happen until they have clocked out and gone home.

Who can blame them?

If people lived longer – 200 years, say – real fixes would begin immediately. Two centuries increases the chances that you'll witness a doomsday.

Interested in global warming now?

Free Whole Foods for All People

Let's review.

The simplest solutions to basic needs that eliminate fear of loss for billions of people get halted and thrown back into debate because a couple in Florida weeps in front of their home while a CNN camera records them saying "This will destroy our lives and everything we've worked for."

This would happen as free oranges began to sink in.

People must – and will naturally - arrange themselves to any new order when that order brings unquestionable positive change. Attempting to halt the Free Oranges for Everyone Forever policy would be just plain dumb when the only change made – the only one – is customers don't need to pay for the oranges. No other changes to the supply chain of oranges, other than more planting. Every check down the line that was there before remains paid.

"By who?"
"Government. They have it. Just have them clear the checks."
Did I hear someone's going to get hurt? Start a fight? You? For what? Free oranges? What do you care what the government owes anyone or if they have money or not? Doesn't affect you. We're all just warned that it affects us. So we keep our books balanced. Still mad? Go ahead then. Yes, you'll get into a fight. What does your fight have to do with free oranges? You're a trouble maker? Guess what? Millions people don't need police or prison to take care of people like you. Particularly at a produce stand.

Critics claiming no natural adjustment to civil order would take place, and that instead chaos would ensue from a declaration there is free food for all, need only look at those individuals who believe that people receiving unemployment pay are not interested in working. The charge that people would not work if they were given enough money to live is a flawed and impossible question.

The reality is people would begin to work on only the things that interest them if they were given enough money to live. Just ask a person criticizing unemployment compensation (or the idea of not having to pay anything to live) if nothing at all is what they would do under the circumstance. Human pride and ambition developed under the former man made model of needs-delivery would retain the kinetic energy to motivate people long enough for curiosity to set in and personal motivations for work surface and reorder productivity and commerce.

The future, the revolution, the change, will arrive at the same rate of speed as today arrived, and yesterday. There is no solution that is one thing we can look at. A plan cannot be overlaid on people's indoctrinated fear of loss. The change has to be organic from our behavior, and we must be free to exercise access to what it takes without being preoccupied with what should have been the question to begin with.

Sure they'll be a few skirmishes and all-out fights, a little broken glass, and maybe a few deaths. But that breaks out at soccer games and we don't say soccer was a bad idea.

Why do we think we have to wait until we have a perfect plan before we take even one step? That's not the way it was built, and it's not the way it's going to change.

Monumentally Agile Retards

"You see, the very reason Mankind is the dominate animal on the planet, the reason we've achieved possession and command of so much, is that we don't get the same sense of satisfaction from things close to us, objects in our circle of existence, as other animals on the Earth do. For us, as a species, objects that are beyond our grasp, far away from us, trigger an attraction response usually reserved, in the rest of the animal world, for objects near to us. It's a genetic retardation that's led us right to the top of the food chain. Only able to experience a sense of peace when we're exploring something new or gobbling something up. All other animals find satisfaction within the environment around them, never feeling the inner need to develop language or teach their offspring anything more than how to survive by example and the bounds of their territory. On the other hand, Mankind's genetic defect prevents us from finding satisfaction with anything around us, anything comfortably ours.

Only objects and ideas not yet inside our control have any attraction to us at all. So we continually strive forward towards the next anything, making us monumentally agile and capable retards, always involving ourselves in the new, but living in pain, so much destruction in our wake. So much forgotten."

Status Living and the Great Outdoors

Consider the last time you went camping, and hopefully anyone reading has.

Everyone had fun and everyone is always ready to go home when it's time or even before. Now think about the good times you remember, the camp fire, marshmallows, beer, music. Companionship. What was the underlying stress? Throughout the event? Answer: Taking care of the stuff you brought from home.

Setting it up, tearing it down, keeping it clean, and worry about running low. All easy chores to overcome until the Status mindsets of value, cost of replacement, wear and tear, appearance, and legality are imported into nature instead of being the troubles you left behind. The underlying stress created by considering the camping gear home furnishing and maintaining it accordingly is a high to Status, who don't like to think of their equipment as slowly crumbling disposable play-survival tools you should destroy camping and buy again next year.

Suddenly camping becomes not a rejoining with nature but instead an exercise in beating it back.

Status brought to nature. A military obstacle course in battling loss.

Intelligence

Homelessness Just Got a Whole Lot Smarter

I got smarter at Baseline.

My studied estimate? Easily 30 percent smarter.

Note I didn't use the word "intelligent."

Smarter.

Jumped up one day and there it was. Zero delay in recalling names of people, cities, songs, rarely used proper nouns like quiver and rotunda, and grammatical modifiers that conveyed my thoughts perfectly in real time as I spoke. Without search or indexing, my use of lazy conjunctive generalizations like "that thing" and "that place with the bikini-clad snow team" was relieved by "that caliper" and "Sweden."

Any word I'd ever heard and understood was ready for duty when called up, without effort. On-the-fly upgrades from words like "old" to "vintage" and "stretchy" to "elastic" arrived with no fanfare or change to my speaking tone or volume, no appearance of forcing out ten dollar words over dimes. Conversation just became richer soil for me.

Baseliners I know who are musicians, painters, artists of any kind, craftsman and athletes, all have reported experiencing increased smarts when plying their talents, improvements that took place after they arrived at Baseline. My increase in smarts wasn't accompanied by any supporting physical improvement, like faster typing. The basketballers agreed. They couldn't run faster or jump higher but they read defense better and their winning percentage jumped. Told me they had more fun playing the game too.

At Baseline, comfortably distant from the clutter of media, non-linear conversations I eavesdrop on, and that mental fire always burning wage slaves, I am significantly smarter that I was in Status. Surprisingly, there is little more to be said about being smarter. In Status, I thought becoming smarter would do a lot more for me than it has. Turns out smarts reveals itself at Baseline as more of a varnish applied to enhance and strengthen, and less a new feature that creates.

Added smarts fed my appetite for visual information and I noticed my eyes darted about more. Not Jack Nicholson in *The Shining* darting about, but more a smooth, constant tennis game surveillance.

Boosted smarts might have improved my hearing but there must be a damper we've set on hearing volume – or at least mine - because I noticed no change in volume in respect to increased concentration on sounds, which was fine with me. House volume in my head has always been set just right, and I've never looked for the nob.

Smarter taste buds? At this writing I haven't eaten anything but basic food in half a year, or dined or ordered out so I have no way to benchmark what would be smarter taste. I don't want to pay to satisfy an appetite I'll lose when sour looks start getting flashed my way in a restaurant, and I never think in terms of food delivery anymore. It doesn't even sound appetizing.

Remembrance

You cannot pin pictures of your loved ones up on a Tree where you camp at Baseline, or on the outside wall of any ally you sleep in.

You'll lose them.

Houses and apartments in Status are typically museums of family portraits and framed photos of times and people to remember, some kept safe for generations because time revisions antique craftwork into contemporary art.

Here though Baseliners share precious pics with one another using their smart phones and tablet PCs. Yes, at Baseline too. Wallet photos still abound.

Baseliners comment on your loved ones. If a loved one is ugly, a Baseliner will make a peaceful comment about it. The person with the picture likely knows the beauty index of the child, but just never spoke it in public before. In the other direction, comments about family enter a minefield of bloodline protectiveness in Status. That's why Status prefer to comment on picture frames of others' loved ones, not the pictures themselves.

To show Mom on your wall in Status it needs to be framed. Mom taped or tacked to the wall, or pinned to a Tree in your backyard will appear like you didn't care for Mom's picture – or for Mom herself – even though the only value of the picture is to see Mom. If a Status company saw this kind of sloppy display they would offer you a spare picture frame they have, or buy you one the next time a gift is appropriate. Framing Mom is a Status concern because framing the picture is what Status would do. This illustrates two traits common to all tiers of Status:

1. Optional add-on products to valuables – here, picture frames – are no longer deemed optional when industry mass produces them at an affordable cost for a particular tier. Choice in Status is not based on section, but budget. Everything afforded to your Status tier must be bought when it comes within your budget range.
2. People in Status may see Mom but since there's no comparing families outside of gossip and television shows the attention runs to add-ons like the frame or a photo matte. Show the picture of Mom leveled neatly in a cheap plastic frame to a wealthy Status couple and they'll delight at their wealth advantage recalling the jeweled and polished frames outlining pictures on their walls. If you ever visit their house you won't think their expensive picture frames overdo it. You'll know in your heart that one day you too will be able to afford a costly one for Mom.

Notice how industry is doing nothing here but acting as the name of the business supply chain for frames. It's not making any decisions on which frames look the best, be they pricey or cheap. Industry is just the idea in play for business people to offer items with prices matched to discretionary spending. Toyota's early car customers could only afford a Corolla. As they got better jobs Toyota built for them the more expensive Camry. As they reached a Status level of luxury Toyota build them the Lexus.

What does it say about Status when a product becomes

a must-have essential just because mass production made it affordable? Where is real necessity and conservation or resources in this behavior?

That picture of Mom brings recurring joy. From it arrive memories and conversations and all that Mommy goodness everyone loves. Mom's mean something in life.

Homeless man with nothing to lose

It's not a beautiful story but when I was young the landscape wasn't blanketed by surveillance cameras so committing a crime was a rite of passage.

During my rite of passage a pal of mine who worked with me at a fast food joint stole about $600. The night time scheme was hatched by a delivery driver with a full pouch of money from deliveries all day. He was quitting his job and wanted one of us to jump him in the ally, beat him up, take the money and his jacket then split it three ways later.

We all did our part. Me the one jumping him in a fake robbery screaming "give it up motherfucker" to someone I'd met an hour earlier. My friend and I should have been busted. We had been left in charge. I almost confessed the very next day.

But without much investigation, the cops closed the case the next morning by busting a homeless guy they collared from a pool of defenseless Baseliners on the street. We hear of this all the time. A homeless guys robs this, steals that. So what, right?

But here I was exonerated – well, overlooked - while a man innocent of my crime had been arrested and would face charges. A man I never met. Knew nothing about. Maybe a guy sleeping in a park for a while to save money for a room deposit so he can get back on his feet. Or a man sleeping in a row of bushes not as a fugitive but embarrassed to be seen homeless in a place with little tolerance for it, wanting no trouble. Just wanting to see his kids again. Maybe coming home from a failed attempt at a long distance job. The cops wouldn't have believe any of these scenarios if they bothered to ask. They knew they were likely looking for a patsy and of course they got one. Of course the homeless guy did the crime. That's what they do. Just like all Asian students are smart, and all professional athletes heterosexual. All homeless people are criminals.

All I knew about the man who took the fall for me was that he probably had nothing much with him. Nothing worth anything really. Maybe a ring with sentimental value but mostly discarded stuff.

He was a man with nothing, nothing to lose.

A homeless man with nothing to lose. Just listen to the criminality ooze off.

"Keep your guns ready boys, these fellas got nothing to lose."

Behold, a crazed lunatic or ex-con is created out of mere words.

Why is "having nothing to lose" bolted to criminal behavior? Why are the most dangerous crooks men with "nothing to lose?"

The only time I've seen good guys utter that phrase was when they were heading into some epic final battle and had resigned to the possibility of failure and death. In this context the statement is nonsense. They have everything to lose.

Change the words, change the world.

What's Pop Culture, Dad?

Pop culture is best described as the sweet and liquidly outer layer of the hardened center of primary culture. Pop culture is the yummy and timely expression of a culture at any given time during its primary culture's development, definition or demise. The introduction of pop culture triggers a germination process that spreads the beliefs, enthusiasms, sounds and visualizations of a specific pop culture element across the entire tribe or nation state. Pop culture elements, like the natural elements of a periodic table, effect things alone or in combination with one another. In all cases where there is a release of a pop culture element into a tribe or nation state, a small percentage of that population is going to experience a negative, mutative reaction to the element. Similar to tissue rejection from an organism that has had a foreign body introduced into it, negative contact with pop culture metastasizes a behavior spoilage with the net result being a disconnection from the growth/decay arc of pop culture and a purging of the change mechanism.

Homelessness is therefore the destination internment camp for those in societies suffering from pop culture tissue rejection. A direct correlation can be found between the release of specific pop culture elements and end-host sociopathic mutations genetically suited for homelessness and populated from pools of all age groups and personality types. Homelessness's tapestry of pop culture mutations makes it by default a scorching attack at pop culture.

Direct links to pop culture elements and the hosts mutated into the homeless types described in this book can be traced using a methodology anchored in the forces of Community, Desire, Free Will and Drug Use.

When we hear a balding pundit on MSNBC imagine gangs of thugs backing their pickup trucks to grocery store bins and taking all the oranges for themselves on the first day of the Free Oranges for Everyone All The Time Forever policy what we should all do is use our imaginations to envision how stupid and foolish the thugs who hoarded the look in a few weeks with piles of rotting oranges in their backyards.

Males have a history of getting drunk together after a girlfriend, lover, or wife leave them. I did this with Dean who told me on Columbus Day that Barbara had left him. For the second time. His words were "we've broken up."

I bought a 12-pack of Bud for Dean and me to polish off at a meeting point at 6th avenue and Fulton, next to my old pad the roller rink, so I could listen to any beef Dean wanted to roast over Barbara. Then it would be my turn. A few well-rehearsed and politely reserved barb-less barbs at Barbara, after Dean had her out of him.

People don't block time to listen to Dean say anything, not even where the dope is. Dean does not present a well of confidence, but rather a lack of resources. This is no put down. It's good to have very little information when it saves you from the hassle of combing through bad information added just for the sake of it. You thank Dean for this insight. Like noticing Hummers and Escalades on the road and making the mistake of getting mad at them. Instead you should thank them since Hummers and the Escalades do us a favor by pointing out the assholes on the road circa 2014.

I really wanted Dean to be able to spill it with Barbara that Columbus Day evening. Get the man chest up. Get the bitch off his mind and maybe shed a few tears. I wanted to be the bro trusted to witness if a 12-pack could do the job of Barbara Walters (Not Dean's Barbara). I wanted him to part the clouds for my comments about Barbara, who I privately disliked. That's how it is between friends who shared the acquaintance of a loved, but under different circumstance. There is always more room to work once you know what parts of the room have been cleared.

But instead of investigating Dean's method of closure, I almost killed Lumpy right in front of him. About an hour earlier I'd asked Lumpy to join Dean and me for the get-drunk-back-to-being-a-bachelor-party. Asked him to bring nothing but his scar and muscle-covered self. He had just borrowed my piezo pipe to smoke some speed he'd scored in the bushes near The Conservatory of Flowers. Waiting for the pipe back, I hung out listening to Lumpy inhale and talk rather candidly about things that were important to him. Friends. Psychic communication. Drumming. People not wanting anything. He smoked like it was his last gasp of air. Abandon Submarine.

"Dan, it's so cool that you stand there and listen, and enjoy and be my friend while I get high. And don't ask for any of it. You're just here," he told me.

That was when I invited him to Dean's breakup party.

Before I nearly killed Lumpy right in front of Dean, who was frozen, terrified, Lumpy mumbled something that developed into a complete thought within his meandering and steadily meaner escalate. He hadn't given back my piezo pipe, so I asked for it again and this came out of him:

"You are painting too rosy of a picture of this place." That sentence was A-Plus articulate coming from a Lumpy head so often beaten to a salt that it had become lifeless brine.

Lumpy sneered inches from my face. He shivered. He didn't bulge with dangerous anger. It was a shiver. He was high as a kite. His teeth chattered for an instant. Fists clenched, the bike he rode leaning behind him against his denim-clad rear.

He was shivering. He was afraid. Lumpy. Lumpy, was scared when he appeared the most threatening, about to strike. No one I knew had ever dared get as close as I was to Lumpy when he was mad at them, or mad at something. Maybe he didn't have my pipe, was beating himself up for it. But then he mentions the book. How the fuck would he have known anything about the book, much less the book's angle.

At budged towards him, inches. I didn't want to talk about the book.

"Give me my fucking pipe back, Lumpy! I don't give a fuck about anything else."

Lumpy started to zone out as I yelled at him. He didn't know what ground he was standing on suddenly. Lost concentration. I was still breathing down him, ready to smash my cane across his head, then run.

He didn't want it from me. I knew that. Not about a pipe. But it was too late for him not to try and bring it on. He wanted any reason to hit me as hard as he could. He wiped his face quickly with both hands open. Blinked real hard.

"You know I'm about to get all Lumpy on you," he said shaking his head. "You are painting a too rosy picture of this place."

So Lumpy waits for you to be frightened by his ability to stare madly into your eyes like he's already smashing you. But what's really behind those eyes is a prayer that you don't attack him. Lumpy and I had enough shared good times between the two of us to weaken his rage the more I kept talking.

"Lumpy this is bullshit. We're supposed to be here for Dean. Not you freaking out! Keep the fucking pipe!" I screaming in his face.

Friendship exposed a weakness in Lumpy that almost led to getting his ass kicked by me, a 50-year old writer who needs a cane to walk. A homeless man with nothing to lose. I was about to kill him if I had to. I could not turn my back. He started to rant about how I never bought him any food and screamed for me to count how many things I'd bought for him in the last week. I bought him food practically every day.

"What have you given me in the past week? Huh?"

Screaming louder. "What have you given me? Huh?"

No one, much less a bunch of $40,000 a year cops and a pair of $80,000 a year detectives, would give a fuck if this asshole tough guy bar bender and shitty drummer lay dying in his own blood on the corner of 6th Ave and Fulton. A dead Lumpy would close a lot of open cases for the SFPD, having a recognized brute to point the fingers at. One who tells no tales.

Lumpy's litmus test was "too little anger equals suspicion."

"Why are you happy in a place where you're supposed to be unhappy? You cannot be happy. Somethings... You. You."

Lumpy growled, lifted a leg over his bike and road away into the park's darkness.

Barbara's plans for herself at Baseline make Don the Traveler's insistence that some livery cab is always on the way to pick him up appear downright feasible. The abysmal condition of Barbara's eroded Status compass makes her permanently out of place everywhere. Barbara doesn't think matters through, so she's only black ahead. She's just as chronically maladjusted and tense at an AA meeting on Waller Street as she is on a blanket on Hippy Hill lying next to Dean and telling me "Time flies when you have absolutely nothing to do."

She says so wearing an expression that clearly displays her lack of interest in doing anything.

Barbara is a born victim. A former night shift banking accountant dealt out by a reduction in paperwork. She misses friends who have distanced themselves from her homeless condition. She is out of ideas. Misses her cat.

For his part, Dean has never demonstrated a posture resembling finesse. Dean's thoughts and emotions are directly connected to his physical reflexes. When you holler out Dean's name at night when you see him walking across the street and Dean cannot see you, he will twirl around with his hands flailing in the air so anyone within distance can see that he is totally confused. Why the dramatics?

Dean will crumple up something you ask him to take good care of. Barbara wanted a fancy, illustrated label removed from a wine bottle so it could be hung as art in their tent. Barbara gave the bottle to me at the library. Dean would come fetch the removed label, so I let him take it off. Not me.

"Dean, Barb wanted the label for show. To hang up. That's why she gave it to me. Don't just freakin' rip it off the bottle. Look at it. It's felt paper, family label, nice art, that's why she wants it."

"No I got it," he claims.

I ask the librarian to help Dean find a plain sheet of paper so he can flatten the slightly ripped, still adhesive label to it instead of folding the label on itself which was his unthoughtout plan.

This label incident was shortly before their second breakup. Upon her phony entrance to Baseline Barbara just as quickly departed to some mental edge of town where permanent twilight has set in. Bad heroin, crack, booze, beatings. Her epic failure to find solace at Baseline was equaled only by her startling misuse of her own visible potential. Barbara is a strangely beautiful woman. Quiet, like she's a seventh grade math teacher with a body aged 60 and a habit aged 30. Barbara never looks like she belongs where she is.

She's not a Baseliner. She's not Status. She is not homeless. She's a person who advertises herself like a finished product, so she's comfortable, or confused by the likelihood she may never be left alone again. Gone are the walls that hid her complex gear box.

Barbara is the sell-side of Baseline/Status limbo. The buy-side consists of limbo-landers like Don the Traveler, the hippy truck guy, the crazy library woman, and hundreds who still not dare leave their cars for the serenity of Baseline. A fingernail still etched in Status.

Why You Can't Help People (Reason No. 69)

You are woken in the dark. She tells you she is lost and afraid. That her guy smacks her around.

You recognize Barbara's voice. She's drunk.

If you open your mouth and say to her "You have to take care of yourself sweetheart, you can't hang with losers like that who punch women" know that she will return to them soon, and when she is mad again it will be you she uses against them, the guy who said you all were losers, the guys whose problem it has now become.

During the cold nights of July everyone in the park and I would listen to Dean and Barbara, then in better times, scream conclusions at one another louder than either needed to hear.

I loved listening to these terribly boring arguments because it was always like catching the last seconds of an auto race just as you enter the TV room with an armful of snacks you would like to set down but instead hold onto until the race is over.

Dean can scream "Fuck!" amazingly loud. One word the strength of a complete, run-on sentence.

"No, fuck you! It's over!"

Dean: "Ahhh!!! Enough!! Ahhh!!"

"You know..! Don't... Listen to me you fucking..!

"Fuuuuuuuuuuuuuuuuuuuuuuuuuuuuuuuck!!!!!" and you could hear the air emptying out of Dean's lungs.

Lumpy couldn't stand it. He reappeared, this time walking. Then he slithered across the pavement to pick up full beer cans bought for Dean's breakup party. Beer cans

Lumpy himself kicked from the cardboard 12-pack container after I told him "Calm down, Lumpy, OK? This is Dean's night here."

If he got close again my aim was knife from the cane into his thigh, either one, then the second he wrenches in pain strike a full blast right fist upper into his goddamn lovable face, blast him to the ground, then take out whatever is left of him while I'm still standing. But these actions from me were just imagination on a wave of disappointment and disgust. Lumpy had fled on bike from someone who did not show fear of him.

He put the beer cans in his backpack and placed something on the ground as he stormed away, like he was embarrassed. He screamed as he left, of the piezo pipe:

"I was going to give it back in five minutes...!"

"Then why didn't you just say that you dumb motherfucker before I fucking killed your stupid ass."

Multimedia

I get excited when I think about Baseline Economics and its reality and promise for each of us, perfect for a 2-minute video shot from the cheapest phone and uploaded to You Tube seconds after the recording light goes out.

Butcher demonstrated this well-known function to me one morning atop the high plank of Hippy Hill when I was drying socks and boxers after washing them in the sink of the tennis club restroom. This 2-minute video was of me, introducing myself and Baseline Economics and this book as quickly and as simply – and urgently – as possible. Blah. Blah, blah, blah, blah.

"See, there you go," Butcher said, holding his smart phone up for me to see as if it was proof.

"You just uploaded it to YouTube?" I asked like it was new to me. You should always allow people to be proud of themselves first. Less important details later.

I watched it on Butcher's phone, not YouTube. I'd lost a lot of weight.

Butcher nodded. "Just like that," he said.

Butcher said he had a daughter attending Harvard Medical School afforded by the profits he realized from selling pot. The best pot on Hippie Hill as a matter of known fact. He slept in a tent he kept loaded with camping gear in a spanking new pull-behind stroller that attached to a bike.

He'd been showing off the features of his smart phone to me that morning. Now I was really interested because I wanted the video of me to post on a Facebook page. I never found the clip on YouTube. I looked for it on a library PC that day. Never found any possible trace of it on every possible key word you'd think of after knowing everything about a person. The next day Butcher told me he lost his phone, and he fumbled to explain why it wasn't on YouTube. He explained it wrong but what he tried to tell me was that the source file (my video) was resident in the client hardware (his phone) which YouTube accessed to play the clip, rather than hosting it on their site, as if Butcher's phone was the server.

Yeah. Right. Baseline technology savvy.

I thanked him. Nothing else. Butcher's great.

I bought a video camera from a kid I yelled at for falling asleep while I negotiated the purchase with him. Literally nodded off in mid-sentence before we got to price. It was a perfect Sony Stupid Cam, but had no charger. I didn't check to see if it had replaceable batteries. A mistake. When its battery died, a day before I asked Dean to hold it steady while I spoke a few encouraging words about Baseline, the Sony stayed dead. I couldn't find a charger that matched it in time for the shoot. It didn't matter. Dean and a musician named Ulysses who I'd invited to play bumper shot music for the videos, never showed up.

I then asked Dean to use his Apple laptop to shoot the videos, him holding the computer in his hands, walking.

Okay. I asked Ulysses again to show up and provide music for the clips.

This time they both showed.

Dean was able to shoot one video before the laptop batteries drained. The footage shakes like The Big One and the audio is blanketed by the sound of Dean breathing heavily and swallowing in audible dry gulps. Ulysses was toasted five sheets to the wind, beer firmly in hand, expansive patch leather jacket studded with razor sharp spikes all the better to hug you with. He'd brought with him a small mouth harp which made the sound you hear when Boss Hog's police car appears down the dirt road packing nothing but trouble. Ulysses wouldn't stop playing when I began speaking. Just wailed on oblivious to what Dean and I were trying to do. I asked Ulysses to remember what Paul Shaffer did when Dave began to talk.

"Dude, listen to me, what does Paul Schaeffer do when Dave stops talking? What does he do? Or not do?"

"Novel Don," Ulysses slurred in his hefty voice. That's what he called me, by the way.

Dean's dog starts barking feverishly, louder on track than Dean's breathing. The mutt's panic terrifies Ulysses, who's built like he bends iron rods all day for a living.

"Novel Don," Ulysses repeated. I had no idea if he'd remember any of this, swaying, staring aimlessly through black wrap-around sunglasses.

The dog kept barking. The Apple hit the sand.

I expressed my frustration with getting these dopey video clips done with Amy, a girl who was lifted from homelessness by San Francisco's Homeless Outreach Team and given free housing through a Section 8 voucher which deducts rent cost from general disability payments. Free rent and about $300.00 per month in discretionary cash, plus $210.00 a month in food stamps. Tell me there is no social safety net. Balls.

"It's like I'm surrounded by incompetence," I

complained to Amy. The footage looks and sounds like it would if someone were walking around with the laptop not realizing that it's recording. Jesus."

A curl of Amy's lovely dark hair tumbled to her beautiful shoulder as her expression awarded a curious tilt of her courageous brilliance. It was the Italian in her. I'd only known her a short time, ran into her on Haight Street, eyes locking, instantly a new day, a new road presents itself, the heart stops.

"Sure, I'll do it," Amy said. "I can use my phone, right?" Why do we act dumb to the operations of technology products we own?

"Thank you, God," I rejoiced, suggesting a location near her apartment instead of way out in the woods. "What I was thinking was the Panhandle, just a block that away. It's quiet. No traffic. And I'll buy you lunch."

I'd fallen in love with her. If there was such a thing as satisfaction Amy was summoning it up from me.

It takes living an epic love story to recognize a new epic love story. That's what I'd pegged for Amy. Love story. I'd seen so little of her since we met, but with each interaction between us the volume of affection shared became breathtakingly more urgent.

She shies back from kisses because I told her I try to grab as much of a person that I love as I can when I get the chance to embrace them. She actually took me seriously instead of cutely. Crap.

She also claims to be coo-coo and unfit to be my girlfriend due to manic episodes she claims rear their ugly head inside her when she feels like she is surrounded, both emotionally and mentally. Crap.

But how lovely Amy dresses the weariness of the world when she smiles at me, reaching for my hand in our soft red San Francisco sunset. In the cartoon light that is a San Francisco night, only a drifting playful lock of hair from her happy wool hat would keep me from losing my train of thought in Amy's gorgeously attendant Earth brown eyes.

"You OK, Dan? You're quiet today."

Casual ease, bohemian aura, Baseline scent, love on the wing, fantastic text writer who employs snappy grammaticism, Amy is a total mystery.

We walk to her doorstep. I don't want to talk about videos. Time with Amy is too precious.

"Don't worry about the details of this thing. We can work everything out when we shoot. Say noon? Tomorrow?"

"Noon? Tomorrow?"

For some reason I have absolutely no way to describe what Amy said to me after that sentence. Her speech was a Bingo tumbler of I want to sleep late I owe myself rest I won't be available in the morning I have a prescription to pick up I won't be accountable for this thought. But it sounded and felt like a yes resisting affection.

I bought a video camera for $4 the next morning from the recycler, Tree. A lanky ex-con sporting arms long enough to reach all the way to the bottom of Sunset Scavenger's four-foot high plastic waste bins. Tree gave me a Minolta. Should work with new batteries. Wanted it just in case Amy forget to delete enough phone memory to accommodate our video length. The story of the Minolta was like most discarded technology in Apple land – Something free from a trade show bag.

The next day Amy walked past where I waited at the Panhandle. She said hi to me. She forgot the date. Tomorrow.

"But that's what Sunday is for, right?" she said.

Oh well. At least she remembered and still wanted to help shoot the videos. Excellent. The piece of shit Minolta didn't work anyway. Back to her equipment we'd go.

"There's a reason people throw things away in the garbage," Amy told me sympathetically, her arm on my shoulder.

She was going to be there.

Sunday arrived with this text from Amy:

"Hi Dan, I'm gonna shoot for 3pm but it may be 4pm. I'm gonna charge my phone... and clean it out too. That'll take a little time. It's pretty full!"

All I wanted to do was hear from her. "I can bring my computer too so you can add the files to a Zip drive if you have one. Lemme know!"

She also had to get a prescription filled. She ended her message with "ha, ha. I hate being in pain. Anyway let me know about the computer."

I sent a text asking her to meet me somewhere closer to her. The paid time on my phone ran out. The text was not sent. Amy said she did not get it. She did not appear. I was in a rut the next time I saw her.

"That's all I wanted, some dumb three minute videos of me just talking about the book. Far from rocket science. You didn't get that text I sent about changing locations?"

"No."

"Yeah, so we could shoot them fast and get it over with. It would have been fine. The web site's going to shrink the shots down to a media player window. It's not like we'll be projecting them on a big screen. They'll get sharper."

Amy was silent. She looked up at me from her station a few inches shorter. Her expression was surprise. Awkward, unhappy surprise. Like a surprise party on a Monday night. She slowly shook her head, looking me right in the eyes. Her voice was hoarse getting out this one sentence:

"So... these were real?" Amy asked.

There was a pause. San Francisco is a small town. When noise stops, it falls. She did not realize what a question she'd just asked. I don't think she realized it was a question.

"So... these videos... were real?"

My shoulders sunk. My look silently asked "why?"

She had thought I was full for shit. Like every other incomplete project hatched by Baseliners, hatched by the homeless. A lot of hot air and shitty gear making something that will never be seen, if at all finished.

Amy thought I was just angling in for a date. Who knows if she'd even cared about listening to me make plans. Those silly homeless people and their sandbox of garbage ideas. I had always been nothing more than a homeless person to Amy. Why ask her to explain herself now? She had never believed a single word I said, except about hugging, so why bother saying anything else? I didn't want to hurt her.

"I miss you already," I remember saying.

The park facing side of Kezar Drive is where I stopped walking. A Subaru wagon was driven by, its driver in tears. I leaned against the light pole at the cross walk, looking down at a section of concrete I'd discovered freshly poured eleven months earlier, that I'd knelt down and carved one word in:

Evelyn.

Know Everyone
Depend on No One
Trust at Your Own Risk
Operate Alone

Electric Loser Land

Also by the author:

Escape from Elvis Island
Deliberate
Four Months of Bliss
All Monsters Attack

Hi dan! I heard i fucked up your life last night. The correspondence was stupid and some is as follows. I lost that 4 mins of my life and more due to that douchewaffle, Flipper. Wtf did I do to you?! He asked me to set up a mtg w his step-daughter, Sarah (you saw us meet on Mon eve)...actually he told her I was "looking for an apprentice." News to me!! Then after I tell him shes cool last night, he tells me I can't trust any street kids and to be careful. Then proceeded to call Sarah "wishy washy" and a "flake." So I let him have it about referring ppl to my biz (let alone to work for me!), and having them be irresponsible and stupider than stupid does (and dumber than Flipper, a tad smarter than a pile of rocks tho!). Also mind you, he tells everyone he's staying with me (w/o asking my permission to say so!), and he previously hooked me up w/ another woman who simply HAS dogs, insisting i need a meeting. She doesn't EVEN WALK THEM! She wanted to store yet stuff in my place. To which he responds "that bitch is shady!). So wtf did I do to hurt you dan? I can show you the transcript later if you really want to spend more time on Flipper equating to a fucknut. Definite fucknut. THX for listening, Dan! ?? how are YOU today?! Amy

www.ingramcontent.com/pod-product-compliance
Lightning Source LLC
Chambersburg PA
CBHW060449290526
45791CB00001B/46
* 9 7 8 1 4 9 7 3 1 2 3 1 9 *